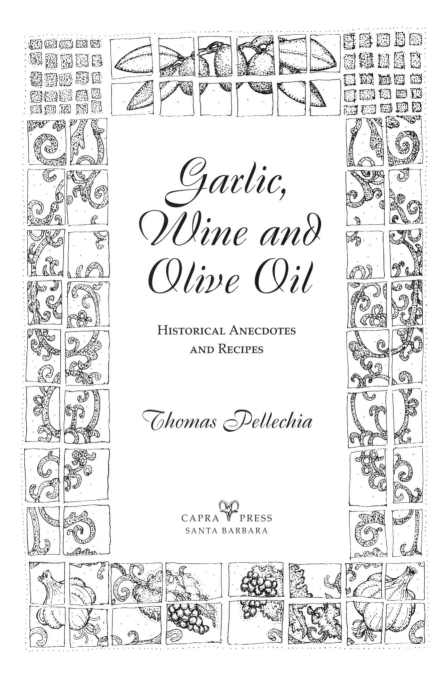

Garlic, Wine and Olive Oil

Historical Anecdotes
and Recipes

Thomas Pellechia

CAPRA PRESS
SANTA BARBARA

Cover photograph, cover design and book design by Frank Goad, Santa Barbara
Illustrations by Peggy Wirta Dahl, unless otherwise noted
Maps and author photo by Anne E. Kiley

LIBRARY OF CONGRESS CATALOGING-IN-PUBLICATION DATA

Pellechia, Thomas 1945-
Garlic, wine, and olive oil : historical anecdotes and recipes / Thomas Pellechia
p. cm.
Includes bibliographical references.
ISBN 0-88496-444-2 (paper : alk. paper)
1. Condiments. 2. Garlic. 3. Wine and winemaking. 4. Olive oil. I. Title
TX819.A1 P45 2000
641.6'382—dc21   00-023719

Capra Press
PO Box 2068
Santa Barbara, CA 93120

To the memory of Mary (Maria) Polzella-Pellechia
1905–1990

Table of Contents

PART VI
Personal Recipe Favorites

Acknowledgments

*T*HE FIRST THREE PARTS of this book recount, in brief, a great deal of history connected to garlic, wine, and olive oil. I could not have done it without the help of others—more specifically, their books. I offer a resounding "thank you" to the authors whose books have helped me both over the years and during research for this book. A few deserve special mention.

For garlic and olive oil history the two most important books in my research were *The Book of Garlic*, by Lloyd J. Harris (New York: Holt, Rhinehart and Winston, 1975) and *The Feast of the Olive*, by Maggie Blythe Klein (Berkeley: Aris Books, 1983). The authors display tremendous passion for the subject, as well as a lively sense of humor. In addition, I got a great deal of help from *Food In History*, Reay Tannerhill (New York: Stein and Day, 1973) and from *A History of Food*, Maguelonne Tousaint-Samat, (Blackwell, 1994). Much of the information in these and other books about food crosses over from book to book, but in each I seemed always to find one more interesting fact the others did not cover, or a different way of viewing the information.

Being a member of the wine industry, I have studied its history over the course of many years and hundreds of books. Yet, I found the following three sources to be indispensable: *Dionysus*, Edward Hyams (New York: MacMillan, 1965); *A History of Wine*, H. Warner Allen (Horizon Press, NY, 1961); and *Wine and the Vine*, Tim Unwin (London: Routledge, 1991).

Other sources that aided me in writing this book are listed in the bibliography.

For the sections pertaining to health and gardening, I cite sources either within the text or in Appendix 3.

For the parts about Brooklyn I called upon memory and a few members of my family. I also recalled the places I have visited, the people who took time to teach me, and the many, many restaurants I have frequented. Finally, to all those who have sat through dinners while I experimented with cooking—thank you is not enough—but thank you.

*A*BIG PARCEL *came for the Professor…a great bundle of white flowers.*

"These are for you, Miss Lucy," he said.

"For me? Oh, Dr. Van Helsing!"

"Yes, my dear, but not for you to play with. These are medicines…but you do not know how. I put in your window. I make pretty wreath, and hang 'round your neck, so that you sleep well."

Lucy had been examining the flowers and smelling them…she threw them down, saying, with half-laughter, and half-disgust, "Oh, Professor, I believe you are putting up a joke on me. Why, these flowers are only common garlic."

—BRAM STOKER, *Dracula*

Introduction

I HAVE A FRIEND who avoids garlic. He claims the only benefit he could possibly derive from eating the Allium is that if the angel of death were to knock on his door the smell on his breath might scare the angel away. If his view of the benefit of eating garlic is true, and I certainly hope so, my friend seems to miss his own point. But I must forgive him his attitude—he is not of Mediterranean stock.

In the Mediterranean, ancient beliefs and superstitions often coexist in conflict. The approach-avoidance relationship between Mediterranean people and the culturally ubiquitous garlic makes the point: garlic is a medicine to cure a plethora of ills; it is an embarrassingly pungent plant; it is a health food; and it is sometimes an agent of the devil, as well as a repellent against evil.

In my neighborhood children were protected from vampires by "The Bag"—a cotton bag, about two inches square, filled with crushed garlic and camphor, that was sewn to our shirts. The Bag was to ward off illness and the occasional wayward evil spirit brave enough to enter our tough Brooklyn, New York environs. It also discouraged gnats, mosquitoes and non-Italians from getting close, all of which we likely construed as evils. The original bag in the Old World, I am told, was concocted with the obnoxiously pungent gum resin, asafoetida, also known as Devil's Dung, to give you an idea of its foul odoriferousness. In deference to the days of the original bag, Brooklyn adults officially dubbed the bag we wore on our shirts The Asafoetida Bag.

I suppose The Bag was responsible for a childhood that was relatively free of evil spirits; once, however, I was awakened when a gangster climbed through our kitchen window to escape the cops in pursuit, but as I was in bed, I wasn't wearing The Bag. I make light of it now, but there must be some truth in the reputed efficacy of The Bag. How else can I explain that I have been Bag-less on every occasion throughout my life when I contracted grave viruses and flu or met with my share of human blood suckers?

I am heartened now that modern science subscribes to many of the less mystical Old World beliefs about garlic, and I am certain that garlic—not the one hanging on my chest, but the one eaten daily—has been my savior for the last half century. A daily dose of garlic is good for the body, and in so being, it is also good for the soul—keeping evil at bay is a plus.

My aim was to write a cookbook focused on garlic. But as I dug deeper into research, a different story unfolded. It spoke to a parallel historical course of three important foods and it caused my focus to shift from merely cooking with garlic to understanding the historical significance of the three foods that were important to my ancestors.

Prevailing wisdom has it that the three most important ancient foods are grain for its protein, wine for its cleanliness and oil for its fats and as a cooking medium. Surely, as they contain the necessary proteins, grains are important. But protein is everywhere, and foods composed of the correct balance of amino acids are completely replaceable by any other foods also composed of the correct balance. On the other hand, many would agree that wine and olive oil are irreplaceable, for their nutritional and medicinal value and for the pleasure they give. But garlic is unrivaled for its reputed beneficial medicinal and bactericidal qualities—it, too, is irreplaceable.

So a case can be made that garlic, wine and olive oil make up a Holy Trinity of Food, which is exactly the case we made in my neighborhood. We of Mediterranean stock are secure in the belief that we discovered the three foods—evidence proves otherwise.

Garlic, grapevines and the olive pre-date human history. And contrary to appearances, cultivation of the three began neither in Greece nor in Rome; garlic and wine were cultivated approximately 8,000 years ago, in the first agricultural civilization, and olive cultivation began perhaps 6,000 years ago. Yet the two great ancient cultures of Classical Greece and Rome were instrumental in documenting the economical, botanical, medicinal and healthful attributes of the three foods, and they were instrumental in centering their cultivation in the Mediterranean. Mediterraneans have earned stewardship over this ancient and healthy triad, which has become a component in our gene pool.

In what I can only describe as a genetic link, I am today unable to free myself from the desire for certain tastes and sensations. The foods I ate as a child helped to shape my identity, and today they bring memories of family and of my old neighborhood, where garlic provided us with safety from evil spirits, wine brought out the good spirit that is inside all of us and olive oil made everything go down easier.

For Brooklyn Italian-Americans in the 1950s suppertime (we never called it dinner) was the family hour. It began at 5 p.m. when the block erupted with the sounds of whistles and shouts from parents calling for us kids to get home to eat. For the next two hours the streets fell silent, overtaken by a heady aroma of garlic wafting from hundreds of tenement kitchens. At the supper table, fathers and mothers talked of the day's trials and victories. And at that table, children were heard as well as seen. It was here where Italian tough-love, that particular brand of affection that comes in a loud, emotional package was meted out to those of us who deserved it. Suppertime was the time to talk things out, no matter how happy, angry or sad the talk was. Suppertime was therapy.

As the aroma of garlic rises today from my kitchen stove I drift back to that supper table of my childhood, in the small, four-room apartment known as a "railroad apartment" because the rooms followed a straight line from one to another. Our kitchen served as the meeting room, the parlor and, most important, the dining room. I hear my young voice trying to rise above the din of older siblings—as the youngest of nine I demanded a lot of time in the limelight. I recall the overwhelming sense of satisfaction I felt after having eaten a tasty, life-sustaining meal, one that for me sometimes included a glass of wine cut with water.

The smell of garlic also brings with it thoughts of an extended family, of uncles, aunts, cousins, neighbors and friends who stopped in to wish us a happy holiday or who shared tales of life in the neighborhood. Gathered in our small apartment, the group gave off a cacophony of life, representing its fun, its sadness and its bustle. Garlic keeps me connected to neighbors and family members who are no longer in my life: to my mother and father; my mother's older sister—and major cause of mom's tribulations—aunt Fannie; my oldest sister, Rose, with whom I spent many hours trading cooking methods (to my wife's amazement, Rose and I talked for an hour one evening on the subject of the proper way to chop garlic and onions); and to two particular neighbors who were instrumental in shaping my passion for food and wine.

Perhaps I got my first taste of wine at the age of nine or ten, but I had been familiar with the smell of wine well before then. Each time I stick my nose into a glass of wine today, to take in its pleasing combination of aromas and nuances, I am taken to November days at the end of harvest, when the last of the grapes came in by truck from California for the neighborhood grandfathers' next crop of wine. For a cheap and sudden thrill a few of us kids would hang around my friend Anthony's small musty cellar on Thanksgiving morning, awaiting our turn to stick our heads into the recently emptied barrels of last year's wine—a deep breath was the price for a ticket to euphoria.

The first time I tasted food cooked in butter I thought something was wrong. What happened, I wondered, to the wonderful nutty flavor, the slight tingle of acidity and the rich viscosity of that luxurious liquid that flowed from the large, ubiquitous tin that appeared in my childhood whenever food was prepared? And a few drops of olive oil into a skillet in my kitchen today takes me back to my teen days. I see myself quietly rubbing olive oil into my scalp, in an effort to moisten and preserve the tight, thick, dry curly hair I inherited and have since lost. But I have never lost the sense of youth that the smell and taste of olive oil represents, that warm irrational belief that we are all immortal. And if we are not, then surely olive oil is immortal, as are garlic, wine, family, societies, history and recipes.

This book, then, is a brief historical account of how three foods—garlic, wine and olive oil—became important in the Mediterranean, coupled with personal recollections that speak to the role the three foods played in my heritage. Being primarily about food, the story includes recipes, both ancient and modern. And with the exception of scant few, the recipes begin with garlic because, notwithstanding the addition of wine and olive oil to the story, in the kitchen I believe you must live by the imperative: Start With Garlic!

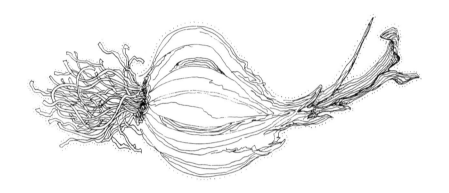

*W*E SHOULD NOT BE WITHOUT IT *in any kitchen, nor leave it out of any food, nor despise it on account of its unpleasant odor.*
—Harawi's Persian Herbal of the 10th century [1]

RECIPE FOR BAKED GARLIC

INGREDIENTS
one large garlic bulb
1 tsp. olive oil
1 tsp. water
garlic baking clay (optional)
a good baguette
1 tbl. sweet basil, chopped

With a sharp knife cut the garlic bulb, horizontally, so that you clip off about half an inch from the top (you are making a pot cover out of the top of the bulb). Drizzle some water into the openings of each clove, followed by a drizzle of olive oil. Put the top back on the bulb and place the bulb into your garlic baking clay (or other stone or clay baking device). Heat the garlic in an oven at 350 degrees for forty-five minutes.

When the time is up, take the top off of the bulb and pop a clove out of its skin. The clove should be soft and aromatic; spread it with a butter knife onto a piece of bread, then sprinkle with basil; the taste is both sweet and nutty.

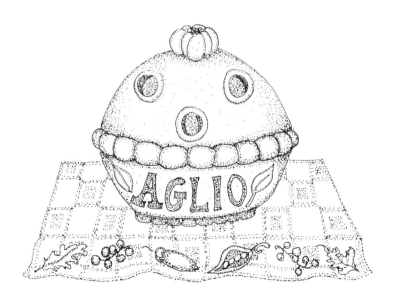

Thomas Pellechia

PART I

The Ancient Perspective

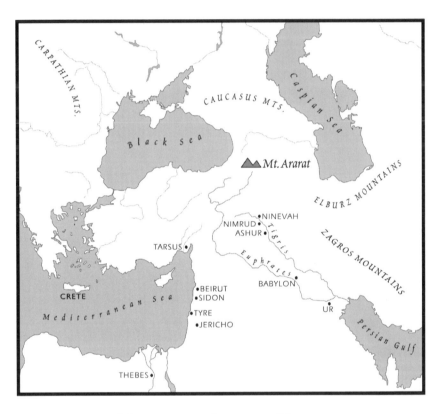

MAP OF THE ANCIENT WORLD

—1—

What Is in a Name

*T*HE ALLIUM PLOT of any garden appears in early spring to look like many rows of the same seedling. A closer look proves otherwise.

About 500 plant species make up the Allium genus. In *The Book of Garlic*, Lloyd J. Harris tells us that "Al" in Allium stems from an ancient Celtic term for *burning*. The most common edible burning bulbs of the genus are onion, leek, chive, shallot and garlic, and though they are similar, they are not alike; you can tell that they are different from one another as their stalks mature.

When the Romans introduced Allium sativum in England the locals likened the tip of its stalk to that of a *gar* (spear), and to them the stalk resembled a succulent wild herb known by its Celtic name, *leack* (leek); they named the plant garleack, and it soon became quite popular.

If you take the garlic bulb you just baked and apply it to the following recipe, you might benefit from a garlic infusion that is so old it perhaps graced ancient Roman and Anglo tables.

INGREDIENTS TO SERVE TWO
2 large garlic bulbs
2 extra cloves of garlic, minced
2 tbl. olive oil
4 cups chicken stock (see chapter 12 for making your own stock)
¼ cup dry Marsala or sherry
2 shallots, chopped
1 tbl. each basil and parsley, chopped
ground black pepper to taste

Bake the garlic bulbs.

Sauté the minced garlic in olive oil along with the shallots. When the shallots are translucent, add the chicken stock, basil, parsley, mashed baked garlic and wine. Simmer for about an hour.

Serve with ground black pepper to taste.

Illustration by Tina Howe

*T*HREE NICKELS *will get you on the subway, but garlic will get you a seat.*

—JEWISH SAYING IN OLD NEW YORK 2

Thomas Pellechia

*A*T THIRTEEN YEARS OLD I was the youngest Fuller Brush man in my neighborhood—actually, I was the Fuller Brush delivery boy. It was my first job ever. I delivered and, if at all possible, collected money for the brushes, lotions, and various household items that my boss, George the Greek, sold to housewives. But George greatly miscalculated our neighborhood. Working class Italian and Puerto Rican housewives did not have the money to splurge on such frivolities on a regular basis. So one day George announced we would visit new territory.

Although a culture shock for this Italian-American teenager to be sitting in the front seat of a car with a man who spoke fluent Greek, the Jewish neighborhood he took me to proved to be a further education. Until then a yarmulke was foreign to me, and I knew nothing of the particular dress code of the Hasidic Jews who dominated the neighborhood. From George's big-finned Chrysler I gazed at boys my age playing in the street dressed in white shirts, dark suits and wearing dark hats—quite unlike the sloppy dungarees and Keds of my turf.

When he returned from his first few sales calls, George told me, in his heavily accented English, "dis iss go-ene to be okay my booey." Each Wednesday for the next few weeks, while George was off selling goods, I was kept quite busy delivering the goods he had sold the week prior.

We worked of course after school hours. Housewives were often getting ready to prepare supper for their hard-working husbands and the brood. In my neighborhood I grew used to the smell of garlic as I made my way up staircases of the large tenement buildings—it was dominant in the thick hallway air. By contrast, the hallway smells of the Jewish neighborhood were normally subtle.

One February week a snowstorm caused George to cancel our usual Wednesday rounds, so he changed our run to Friday, which happens to be the eve of the Jewish Sabbath.

"Take it back," was the most common response to my knock on the door that day. I made no deliveries and George made no sales. But I recall the unusual overwhelming burst of garlic emanating from the bottom to the top floor of the buildings that Friday—today I know why.

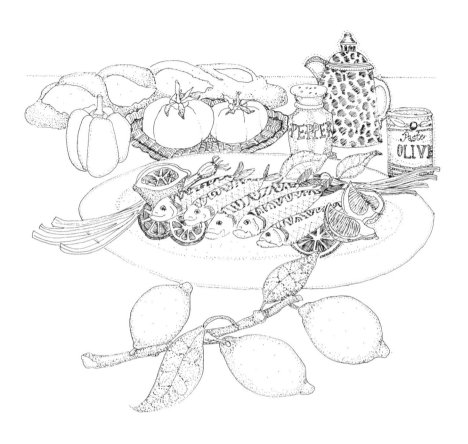

$\mathcal{W}$E REMEMBER THE FISH *which we did eat in Egypt so freely, and the pumpkins and melons, and the leeks, onions and garlic...*

—NUMBERS 11:5 [3]

MONG THE TALMUDIC civil and religious laws of Judaism, is one that tells married couples to reserve Friday evening, the Sabbath, for sexual relations. That law inspired the fifth century BC Hebrew priest and scribe, Ezra, to command the Jews to eat garlic on the Sabbath—because it activates sexual drive.

Jews are also aware of the darkside of garlic's ability to activate sexual appetite. In his book, *Jewish Magic and Mysticism*, Joshua Trachtenberg offers a remedy for those who consume garlic on a day other than Friday and are subject to a surprise attack of urges—it includes pressing your big toes firmly into the ground and then resting the entire weight of your body upon them without leaning against a wall! (3)

The Talmud prescribes garlic or onion skin preparations to treat inflammation of a wound; it also refers to garlic as a means to stave off hunger, provide the body with warmth, brighten up the face, destroy parasites, inspire love over jealousy and a treatment for gynecological and menstrual problems. In what later became the basis for herbalism, ancient Jewish physicians believed that garlic put the body's healing functions into full throttle.

Jews seem always to have cultivated garlic, but they were not the first to do so.

SCHOLARS BELIEVE garlic originated in west-central Asia, as a wild plant that thrived even before the development of civilization; its cultivation spread by way of ancient trade routes. Garlic was one of the cultivated crops of the Sumerians of Mesopotamia, some 8,000 years ago in the city of Ur. Early Sumerians were great grain and plant life eaters. They ate barley, wheat, millet, chickpeas, lentils, beans, cucumbers, lettuce, cress, mustard, turnips, onions, leeks and garlic. In this earliest civilization, both agrarian and urban, the annual harvest was a sacred and most important event.

The ruler and spiritual leader of a Mesopotamian community appointed his priests the responsibility for crop cultivation, harvesting, distribution and storage. To be efficient at the job, the priests devised an inventory control system in the form of pictographs scratched into rock or clay. The etchings identified individual items and their quantity and they formed the basis for the first written expression of diverse thoughts and ideas, known as cuneiform. The priests became the intellectual class of Mesopotamia. For the next few millennia they were responsible for documenting, in cuneiform, botanical, medicinal and culinary matters.

4,000 years ago Babylonians warehoused thousands of bushels of garlic for its special place at their dining table, and when these Semitic people migrated they brought garlic cultivation with them; scholars at Yale University discovered three Babylonian tablets from this period that include a recipe for game meat stew cooked with onions, leeks and garlic.

Next door to Babylon, the Levant became home to Syrians, Palestinians and Phoenicians, all of whom revered garlic. The Phoenicians exploited centuries old trade routes from Mesopotamia to China with access to a wide variety of foods and spices to buy and sell. As the first commercially successful sea-faring peoples, Phoenician itinerant merchants did more than any previous culture to bring exotic commodities from the East to the West. Among the most important of the commodities on board their ships was of course an ample supply of garlic, both as food and to treat various illnesses that regularly attacked sailors during long journeys.

*M*AKE A WHEAT BREAD, *add large amounts of absinthe, and a container of garlic with beer and fat ox meat... the patient's eyes and nose (will) open, leading him to a bowel movement.*

—TABLE 37, CODEX EBERS [4]

Garlic, Wine and Olive Oil

*O*NE OF THE MOST IMPORTANT trading partnerships of antiquity was the one between the Phoenicians and the Egyptians, and it is certain that from this relationship Egypt was exposed to new foods from the East. The Egyptians left lots of information about their culture but apparently scholars have found little information about their food. Much of what is known about the ancient Egyptian diet—that they viewed garlic as a god—was reported by the fifth century BC Greek, Herodotus, and the first century AD Roman, Pliny.

Herodotus studied the Pyramid of King Cheops at Gisa built almost 5,000 years ago. He reported that it took twenty years to build the Pyramid, plus in excess of $2 million (in today's money) worth of vegetables, including garlic. Inside the Pyramid garlic provided royalty with sustenance in the afterlife, and its powerful anti-fungal properties made it important material for the mummy's wrap.

They may not have left many dinner recipes but the Egyptians were the first to record and practice formal medicine. According to E. von Strubing's *Garlic in Ancient Times*, published in Germany in 1967, the Codex Ebers, an Egyptian papyrus of about 1500 BC, listed nearly two dozen therapeutic formulas with garlic as a cure for gastrointestinal disorders, headache, heart problems, weakness, bites, worms, tumors, and problems in the menstrual cycle and in childbirth.

Yet Egyptian priests disdained garlic both because of its smell and because they saw its adoration among the throngs as a threat to their authority. Egyptians with garlic on their breath were often turned away at the temple doors. This kind of controversy connected to garlic echoes throughout history.

Thomas Pellechia

33

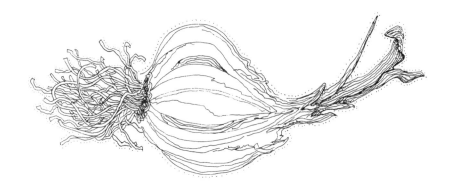

*W*HEN S*US'RUTA has found a special plant he asks the Muni...The holy man answers: 'The Lord of Asuras himself drank the well-shaken nectar. The holy Ianardana beheaded this Lord. The pharynx stayed with the head. Blood drops fell to the ground from the pharynx, and they were the origin of garlic...the Brahmans do not eat garlic since it stems from a corpse...the Creator created garlic to remove the defects of these three juices (the airy, the bilious and the phlegmatic) so that it can heal all diseases...*

—A*NONYMOUS*, 5TH CENTURY I*NDIA* [5]

*G*ARLIC MADE ITS WAY throughout Asia as a result of trade routes. On the sub-continent the Indian Brahman class shunned the potent plant. Like Egyptian priests, the Brahman considered the ignorant who believed in garlic to suffer from illusions and easily swayed from their spiritual path. But the lower caste of Indian culture saw garlic as both an important food and herbal medicine. When the Indian physician Sus'ruta wrote that garlic was created to "heal all diseases" he simply echoed an ancient Asian sentiment.

From Chinese texts scholars found that garlic was in use in China at least as early as 2,000 BC, both as medicine and as food. As medicine, garlic was used as a sedative, and for a variety of respiratory illnesses.

The ancient Chinese believed that God sent them garlic as a gift to clean up their dinner meat. In Marco Polo's *Travels*, the explorer wrote of his thirteenth century trip to the Yunnan of western China. There, he saw people cut the liver from an animal, chop it, marinate it in garlic sauce and then eat it raw.

Perhaps we should not go so far as the ancient Chinese but many cultures since ancient China subscribed to the same beliefs regarding the anti-microbial benefits of garlic. Modern scientists have studied, and now confirm, many of those ancient beliefs; some of their recent findings appear in chapter 11.

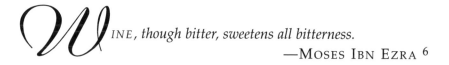

$\mathscr{W}$INE, *though bitter, sweetens all bitterness.*
—MOSES IBN EZRA [6]

—2—

Legends and Origins of Wine

*K*ING JAM-SHEED, *founder and ruler of the city of Persepolis, came to look with disfavor on a former beauty of his harem and so he banished her. She became despondent and went for a long walk.*

She came upon the king's warehouse where he stored his favorite food—grapes—in a jar marked "poison" so that no one else would eat them. She saw that the grapes had broken down into a liquid so she decided to end her life by taking a cup of the king's poison.

But when she drank from the cup her spirit was revived and life took on new meaning. Excited by what had happened, she brought a cup of the liquid to the king who upon tasting it took her back into his harem, and decreed thereafter that the purpose of growing grapes in Persepolis would be to make wine.

—ANCIENT PERSIAN LEGEND [7]

*T*HE TRADE RELATIONSHIP between Egypt and the Phoenicians was centered in the Levant, in the area we know today as Lebanon. Early Phoenicians settled here at around the same time that Egypt had colonized the region for its cedar wood. The complete Phoenician influence on Egypt is difficult to measure, but it is clear to scholars that Egypt learned about viticulture from the Phoenicians.

Like garlic, wine was one of the Phoenicians' prized trading commodities. Scholars believe the root of the near-universal word for wine is derived from a Phoenician Semitic word that specifically referred to fermented grape juice. In the Semitic Hebrew language today it is *yain*; in Arabic, *wain*: in the romance languages, *vin, vino, viña, vinho*; in German, *wein*; and in English, *wine*.

The Phoenicians ultimately established viticulture and wine trading ports at the great cities of Tyre and Byblos, and from here Egyptian royalty imported much of their wine until about 2000 BC, when they established their own sophisticated viticultural regions. After that, Egyptian princes and high priests took control of wine at home, and often engaged in the prestigious enterprises of viticulture and winemaking. Researchers in the nineteen twenties found in King Tut's tomb wine amphorae complete with labels that included the vintage date, the winery location and the name of the producer or winemaker.

Laborers on the Pyramids were among the few Egyptian commoners who got to taste wine, which their masters treated them to during festivals or on certain prescribed occasions. Otherwise, Egyptian commoners drank barley beer or the juice of fermented dates.

Some scholars speculate that Biblical Canaan and Phoenicia were one. If true, the theory explains why, when they thought they would never cease to wander in the desert with Moses, the Jews expressed a longing for the great Egyptian wine they had known. For it was from their trade with Phoenicians that Egyptians learned to produce superior wine, and many of the Jews subjugated in Egypt were descendants of Esau, who married and settled in Canaan. In the Old Testament's Book of Numbers, Chapter XIII, sections 17,18, 20 and 23 all hint at a thriving Canaanite wine culture.

But neither Phoenicians nor Egyptians nor Jews were the first to practice viticulture.

Some claim wine is the oldest beverage of civilization. This is not so: first comes barley beer, followed by brews made from the date palm and pomegranate, then comes wine. But this fact says little of wine's antiquity. In 1997 archeologists found in the Zagros Mountains of Iran drinking vessels with grape wine residue, confirming that wine was consumed east of Mount Ararat at least 7,600 years ago. Yet, archeologists also know that grapes pre-date agriculture, and since grapes can ferment without human intervention, it is certainly possible that wine pre-dates agriculture too.

Grape seed remnants have been discovered in Paleolithic European caves, but no one can say whether the grape seeds were the result of a delightful dessert of fruit after a filling meal of wild game, or whether the presence of grape seeds signifies that wine accompanied the meat dish. Those who know how wine is made should have no trouble accepting the possibility that a pile of grapes, thrown into a corner of the cave, perhaps in a warm spot, might have been forgotten by the cave-master, and within hours began to deteriorate and ferment. But if wine existed in Paleolithic times, we are left to wonder why the delay of more than 2,000 years before the appearance of viticulture—there is an explanation.

Wild grapevines produce either male or female flowers. Vines with only male flowers produce no fruit; vines with only female flowers produce fruit only when the rare pollination of flowers between male and female vines is successful. In order for grapevines to produce fruit year after year, and in order for humans to produce wines consistently, the vines needed to be rescued from the wild—to be cultivated. The ancients needed to discover, single out, plant, cultivate and duplicate the rare hermaphroditic vines that produced both male and female flowers, which Mesopotamians ultimately learned to do after they decided to plant gardens and to stay put.

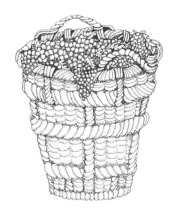

A METHYST *it bore as its fruit,*
Grapevine was trellised, good to behold,
Lapis lazuli it bore as grape clusters,
Fruit it bore, magnificent to look upon...
—FROM THE EPIC POEM *GILGAMESH*, C.18TH CENTURY BC [8]

ODAY THE GRAPEVINE GENUS, Vitis, comprises at least 8,000 different grape varieties, of which one cultivar, Vitis vinifera, produces arguably the best table wines. Vitis vinifera is referred to as a European grape species, yet its ancestry is in the wilds of the Transcaucasus, in the vicinity of Mount Ararat, a fitting fact that ties nicely into the Biblical story of Noah who, upon reaching the dry land of Ararat, first gave worship and then planted a vineyard.

The story of Noah is echoed, in slightly different form, in the epic Babylonian poem of Gilgamesh of about 2000 BC. The two stories, plus archeological discoveries, confirm that floods were common in ancient southern Mesopotamia. As shelter from the frequent floods, southern Mesopotamians constructed man-made mountains on which to plant winegrapes. But it was the special and rare northern Mesopotamian wines that sparked greater interest, and it was to Babylon and to the Levant that much of the wine was shipped.

The same Babylonians who warehoused thousands of pounds of garlic bulbs also housed an ample supply of wine. But the center of Babylon had no viticulture so the wines consumed in the great city were brought in by traders by way of the most common route for trade with the north: along the Euphrates and Tigris rivers. This wine trade underscores the earliest importance of a major waterway to viticulture and to trade.

Prevailing belief has it that the first to store wine in wooden casks were the medieval French, but the "invention" was first seen on trade voyages to Babylon from Armenia. According to historian Edward Hyams, in his book *Dionysus*, Mesopotamian traders

Garlic, Wine and Olive Oil

made a circular raft of skin framed out of willow wood. They placed a layer of straw over the skin to protect it from their cargo of wine stored in date palm wood casks. Taking with them one donkey, two men rowed and floated down the Tigris. In Babylon they sold the casks of wine, the straw and the willow frame of the vessel. Afterwards, the men rolled up the skin, loaded it and some provisions on to the donkey and set off for home.

Wine was so important to Babylonian culture and trade that the Code of Hammurabi, about 1800 BC, included that a fraudulent wine seller—one who sold short—would be tossed into the river. The code also said that unruly drunkenness in the neighborhood taverns—operated mainly by women—would be dealt with similarly.

The wine trade between Mesopotamia and Babylon certainly is ancient, but as archeologists have discovered, not as ancient as Mesopotamian wine trade with Persia.

Ancient Persians believed strongly in the spiritual power of wine; traders entered into business agreements only after they had consumed enough wine to give them the spiritual insight to see whether the contract had merit. If a trader did not agree to a cup of wine, the Persians suspected him of duplicity. Of course modern Persia (Iran) is no longer a seat for viticulture, but this situation is merely two decades old.

*S*TILL IN OUR TWENTIES and just three days married, my wife, Anne, and I left the day after Thanksgiving on a plane for Iran, on what was certainly a most unusual honeymoon. The price of food in Tehran was reasonable, and for food and wine people like us it made ours a trip of a lifetime. We could see, first-hand, the ancient connection between food, wine and the Persians, and we made good use of the opportunity to do so. For the equivalent of a nickel or a dime Iranian street vendors sold sweet, flavorful, large char-roasted sugar beets and char-broiled corn on the cob, the kernels of which seemed big enough to gag an elephant's throat. The vendors' set-up resembled that of a peanut or chestnut vendor on the streets of New York City, but the carts were not as upscale.

I paid dearly for my abandon with a severe case of amoebic dysentery after a few months of eating my way around the country. Luckily, I discovered Iranian yogurt and the ever-present yogurt-making shop that in Tehran neighborhoods, as in most villages throughout Iran, was as important as the bread shop (like much of the East, flat bread baked in stone ovens is common in Iran).

A bowl—about 16 ounces of creamy, somewhat loose, unflavored yogurt—sold for the equivalent of ten cents. Fruit or sweeteners, should anyone want to add them, were added at home. Iranians also sold plain yogurt mixed with crushed garlic which, if I was smart, I would have eaten daily from the start. A diet of yogurt's friendly bacteria coupled with garlic's reputed bactericidal action certainly is more appealing as a defense against intestinal problems than the recommended chlorine wash into which we were told to immerse our fresh vegetables.

Tehran is built on a desert plateau with a wide disparity between daytime and nighttime temperatures. The city gets its water by the force of gravity, via gushing rivers and streams that emanate from the meltdown on the snow-capped Elburz Mountains to the north. It is an efficient system designed in the days of Alexander the Great. At an average 5,000 feet above sea level, water flows from the northernmost point of the city to the most southern point, where the city drops to about 3,000 feet above sea level; temperatures between the north and south within the city's

Garlic, Wine and Olive Oil

borders can vary as much as ten degrees Fahrenheit.

The city has no sewers. Wastewater is discharged into underground cisterns or, as in older streets, the mountain water flows down cemented ditches called jubes. It was not unusual to find Iranians of little means washing their bodies, clothes, produce and sometimes relieving themselves in the jube, which is why it was best for us to sterilize fruits and vegetables bought at the open market.

A drink called Ab Ali—God's water—is also popular in Iran. It is yogurt whey sold in recycled soda pop bottles. Clear at the top and milky white at the bottom where the whey settles, a bottle of the drink must be shaken vigorously to mix the liquid with the whey. It is an acquired taste, one of the rare tastes that neither Anne nor I managed to develop during our two-year stay.

In our second year in Tehran we became members of the Tehran Club, a place frequented by ex-patriot Britons. It was modeled after a London club, and so I learned to play squash and to sit in an over-stuffed chair while nursing my imagined malaria with a gin and tonic in the men's bar.

I suppose the Tehran Club was to the British what staying in a Hyatt Hotel might be to traveling Americans: a sense of security and home in a far off place. Outside the club's grounds we were obviously in Tehran, and inside the grounds, by the swimming pool, it was dry, hot and sandy—traits uncommon in England. But inside the club we were perhaps in the financial district of London. The quiet rustle of newspapers from behind large, stuffed leather chairs and the gentle snoring of men perhaps bored by the news was accented by the clinking of ice cubes in a glass. The interior air was rich with colonial snobbery as Iranian waiters and cleaning women bustled throughout, catering to the whims of the clientele. "Bring me a gin and tonic." "Are there any English-written newspapers around?" I haven't a clue as to how or why we Americans were let in.

The club's menu was full of those particularly English delicacies like bangers, kidney pie, and mashed potatoes. But the club was also known for its dishes of fresh Iranian river fishes, broiled in lemon butter with pistachio or almonds, accompanied by garlic-laced chopped potatoes cooked in olive oil and topped with parsley—an

Iranian dish which somehow got by the British censors.

A truly delightful eating experience at the Tehran Club was to sit by the pool and lunch on cold yogurt soup with Persian melon—so simple and yet so wonderfully satisfying.

INGREDIENTS TO SERVE TWO
3 cloves garlic, minced or pressed
1 large cucumber, chopped into tiny cubes
16 ounces of plain yogurt
1 tbl. olive oil
handful of spearmint leaves
a lemon, quartered
one ripe Persian melon, quartered

(It is nearly impossible to find a properly ripened Persian melon in the U.S. At home, Anne and I grow a reasonable substitute in our garden, an Israeli melon called Ogan.)

Mix the garlic, cucumber and olive oil into the yogurt. Serve cold, sprinkled with spearmint leaves.

Give two each of melon and lemon to your partner and take two for yourself. Sprinkle the melon with squirts of lemon. Then alternately spoon out a chunk of melon and a spoonful of the yogurt-cucumber soup.

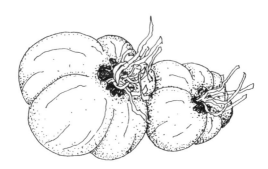

Garlic, Wine and Olive Oil

$\mathcal{T}$HE FAMOUS CASPIAN SEA is about 90 miles north of Tehran, and not too far east of Mount Ararat. Our first of two trips to the Caspian was by car—a trip that took nearly six hours, over a road that wound up the Elburz Mountains to about 12,000 feet in some spots and then down to sea level at its end. Traveling the wildly winding unpaved roads, sans guide rails, at more than thirty miles an hour would have been to flirt with an early demise precipitated by a considerable drop and a few bounces along the edges of rocky mountainsides. But the beauty and history of the Caspian region made the trip worth the risk. Alexander the Great made a similar, but even more time-consuming trip through the mountains to the Caspian in the fourth century BC.

The Caspian Sea is home to three types of big sturgeon: Beluga, the biggest and longest-lived, Osetr and Sevruga, and of course their famous tiny eggs called caviar (khavia is a Turkish word that refers specifically to sturgeon roe).

A long time ago, caviar fishermen preserved their catch in the earth along the seashore as it awaited its delivery to market. Not being from a salty ocean, caviar is comparatively low in salt, which makes it highly perishable. The secret to the success of the fishermen's storage system was the borax found naturally in Caspian soil. Today, borax is not allowed in caviar sent to the United States and parts of Europe, so salting is the preferred method of preservation, which truly ruins the taste of caviar.

Our first taste of premium, unsalted caviar came our way at a British-operated casino. The caviar was quite a reward for leaving behind a few thousand rials at the tables (one dollar was worth about 165 rials in those days). Being more inclined toward wine and less toward spirits, we were pleasantly surprised to learn that chilled vodka pairs well with caviar. But being so close to Vitis vinifera's origins, we were compelled to try caviar with local Caspian-produced wine.

The Iranian religious revolution of 1979 had not taken place yet, so we were lucky to have access to Iranian wine. Northern Iran produced a delightfully crisp, fruity Riesling, with characteristics common to the best German and New York State Rieslings. The wine paired well with the many spicy rice dishes that made up the Iranian daily diet, and its crisp acidity was perfect with the oily river fishes served at the Tehran Club which, happily for us, kept the wine in inventory. But the fine Riesling also made a marvelous companion to caviar-yogurt omelet.

INGREDIENTS TO SERVE ONE
(an omelet should always be created one at a time):
1 clove of garlic, chopped
3 eggs
splash of water
pat of butter
dash of Tabasco
1 tsp. chopped basil
dollop of plain yogurt
small spoon of caviar

Break the eggs into a bowl, add a splash of water, Tabasco to taste and basil. Blend the eggs lightly with a fork to a count of forty.

Sauté garlic in butter in an omelet pan on medium heat. When the butter shows a slight bubbling (do not let the butter brown), pour the egg mix in. Fluff the eggs, dabbing here and there and on the sides, until the sides are cooked, about three minutes. Then fold the omelet with a spatula, cook for a minute and serve on a plate.

Add a dollop of yogurt and a spoon of caviar on top of the omelet.

Serve with a piece of crisp bread, and of course, Riesling.

Garlic, Wine and Olive Oil

*A*LEXANDER AND HIS ARMY must have been as sorry as we were to leave the north of Persia and the Caspian Sea; ancient Greeks were accustomed to drinking white wine. Yet earlier, when his army had sacked and burned Persepolis, Alexander might also have feasted on southern Persian red wine, and maybe it was the one Anne and I tasted and liked.

The wine was bold and forward, and its name was "Yech-hezaar-yech" (1001) and it sold for the equivalent of about $3 a bottle. It reminded of a rich, peppery wine from the French Rhone region (some historians believe the Syrah grape in the Rhone was brought there from Persia). Having never discovered the significance of the wine's name, we left the country with the fantasy that 1001 referred to the year the wine company began in Persia; was it 1001 BC?

Like much of the Near and Middle East, Iran has a national kabob dish—it is called chellow-kabob, and it is as ubiquitous in Iranian culture as hamburger is in ours. We matched chellow-kabob with the peppery 1001 wine, but the dish goes just as well with an equally lush Shiraz or Syrah from any country.

INGREDIENTS TO SERVE TWO
3 cloves garlic, chopped
1 cup of dry red wine and tarragon for the marinade
½ cup of long grain white rice (Basmati)
½ pound of cubed lamb steak (shoulder or leg)
1 large onion, quartered
2 eggs
ground black pepper

Marinate the lamb in wine, tarragon and garlic overnight. When ready to cook the dinner, strain the garlic from the marinade and add it to the water in which you will cook the rice.

Put the rice in two cups of water and bring to a boil, then lower the flame to simmer for about ten minutes, or until most of the water is soaked up by the rice.

While the rice cooks, spear the lamb cubes on metal skewers and charbroil them to your taste.

Turn off the heat and cover to let the rice absorb the rest of the liquid. When the rice is done, fluff it with a fork and place each rice serving into a deep soup bowl in the form of a mound and quickly make an indentation at the top of the mound. Crack and pour an egg into each indentation in the steaming rice; mix the rice and egg and sprinkle black pepper over it.

Place a skewer of lamb on the side of each bowl plus two quarters of onion. Then take a cube of lamb off the skewer, roll it into the rice and egg with a fork and pop the mix into your mouth, followed by a piece of raw onion.

Some Iranians serve chellow-kabob with yellow rice made that way by an addition of turmeric; turmeric rice became popular in ancient Persia to emulate the yellow rice of the Indus that was prepared with the more expensive and rare saffron.

Another favorite kabob dish is called Jubje-kabob. The meat for this dish being lemon-marinated baby chickens. The rest of the recipe is about the same as chellow-kabob, the difference being that the chickens are split in half and then skewered, and that Anne could not bring herself to eat baby chickens.

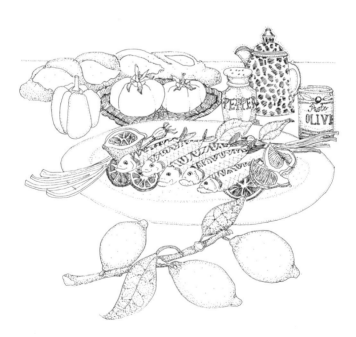

Garlic, Wine and Olive Oil

*O*LD *FRIENDS know what I like:*
They bring wine whenever they come by...
In wine there is a heady taste...

— T'AO CHI'EN, 5TH-CENTURY POET [9]

*O*N OUR WAY TO IRAN, Anne and I spent a four-day stopover in Geneva, Switzerland, where we discovered a marvelous Chinese restaurant called Le Chinois. It was a tiny place located inside an old apartment building. The dining room was arranged to look like someone's living room, and we could locate no kitchen. Yet Chinese waiters were frantically serpentining the tables with trays piled high. The kitchen mystery was solved for us when we noticed a waiter open a set of doors that revealed a small rope-adorned dumbwaiter, out of which he picked up the main course for a table nearby. The waiter yanked the ropes for the dumbwaiter to be pulled back upstairs to, we assumed, the kitchen.

The food was Chinese but it was delightfully infused with French overtones like flowery herbs or even the use of butter in some dishes. The wine, however, was not at all memorable, which had more to do with the difficulty in pairing the dry Swiss and French wines that dominated the wine list with spicy, even sweetened, Oriental food, although many diners were doing it. We drank Chinese beer.

A few years ago in New York City, as I perused the menu of a Chinese restaurant in the fashionable Heights neighborhood in downtown Brooklyn, I noticed a wine bottle with a distinct Chinese label resting on a nearby table of four. Having been searching for wine in Chinese restaurants for many years, I was delighted to order the wine to accompany hot and sour soup, vegetables in garlic sauce and the hot General Tao's Chicken.

Upon its arrival, however, it quickly became evident to me that this particular wine was unlikely to pair with most foods cooked in that restaurant. The already uncorked bottle of dry white wine was a product of Bordeaux, France. Once again, I drank beer.

Knowing that the best wine for spicy Oriental food should be bright and fruity, it seemed a perfectly nutty idea to me that a Chinese restaurant would offer a dry, oak-aged wine with its food. But the idea appeared less nutty after I learned more about the limited history of wine in China.

Vitis vinifera vines were introduced to northern China from Persia during the Han Dynasty, in about 128 BC. But the wine seems to have remained a kind of hobby with the elite of Chinese society, and then it fell out of favor completely. About six hundred years later, Turkish people of Turkestan reintroduced viticulture to northwestern China. Wine then flowed into western China along with garlic and other spices by way of the Silk Road, during trade with Indian, Levantine, Persian and Christian merchants. But the everyday Chinese again seemed uninterested in wine and its trade ultimately died off.

The results of a 1994 study in Japan reported in the British journal *Lancet*, offers perhaps a better understanding of Asian indifference to wine. The study indicated that about half of all Asians suffer from a metabolic inability to convert potentially toxic aldehydes produced by ethanol (the alcohol in wine) into benign acetic acid (which is how most people metabolize ethanol). Perhaps the oriental aversion to alcohol throughout history has been simply a survival mechanism!

The destiny of wine has fared no better in India than it has in China, although there was a time when India, too, produced and traded in wine.

The area we know today as Afghanistan was part of ancient India, and it was the entry point to the subcontinent from the north; after leaving Persia, Alexander's army traversed the treacherous mountains there to enter India. This region of India produced wine in ancient times, and traded it along the Silk Road. Today, however, mostly those of means consume what little quantity of wine is imported into or produced in India.

With the exception of the western Asian cultures of the former Soviet Union, wine is not in the Asian culture—yet. Recent developments show an increase in wine consumption in both India and China.

—3—

Legends and Origins of the Olive Tree

ACCORDING TO GREEK MYTHOLOGY, Zeus awarded Attica to Athene over Poseidon when the two were matched against each other in the assembly of the gods. The prize went to the one who produced the most useful invention to mankind. Poseidon created a powerful and swift war-horse that ascended from the sea; Athene created the valuable oil and wood of the olive tree, which sprung from a large rock known as the Acropolis. Zeus considered Athene's creation and symbol of peace prize-worthy, so he gave a city to Athene and named it after her. In another myth, the olive tree flourished in the Acropolis until invading Persians burned it down; within a few days the tree had sent out new shoots.

In actuality, mainland Greeks were introduced to olives through trade with the Minoans who likely sold olive oil made at the Room of the Olive Press, in the Palace at Knossos, in Crete. At first, the Greeks used the expensive olive oil in cosmetics and for body anointment. By the tenth century BC, olives were cultivated in Greece and soon became a primary and profitable crop. Four centuries later, Solon, the Athens politician, introduced protective legislation pertaining to olive production and sale in Athens, and according to his biographer, Plutarch, he decreed that major plantings of olive trees in Athens would replace grain. Anyone who cut down or damaged olive trees did so under the threat of heavy fines. Such had become the importance of olives to Greek civilization. But as with garlic and wine cultivation, the story of olive oil precedes Classical Greece.

Illustration by Tina Howe

*H*ER AGELESS STRENGTH *defies knaves young and old, for*
Zeus and Athens guard her with sleepless eyes.
—SOPHOCLES, OEDIPUS AT COLONUS [10]

INE THAT MAKETH GLAD the heart of man, and oil to make his face shine...

—PSALMS 104:15

NCIENT CIVILIZATIONS used a lot of oil: it fired their lamps, it was food, it activated medicinal unguents and it was used in spiritual anointments. Although wild olive trees grew in the Levant, the fruit from the thorny plant offered no oil. Mostly, the ancients relied on oils extracted from seeds and nuts. But along the way came the discovery of a means to cultivate and produce an olive tree that was rich in fruit and oil.

Some scholars recognize Crete as the birthplace of Olea europae, citing that the earliest evidence of its cultivation there dates to about 2500 BC. In contrast, evidence exists that olive oil was traded among the Semites of Palestine and Syria and the Egyptians as early as 2900 BC. To add to the confusion, another view of history has it that early Minoans and early Egyptians are one culture, divided only by the Aegean, which the Minoans managed to navigate with ships; if true, olive cultivation in Egypt and in Crete could be even older than 3000 BC.

In any event, olive cultivation began either in the Levant or on an island close by. And whoever it was to first cultivate the thornless, oil-rich version of the olive must have also become rich on the discovery; soon after its introduction, olive oil became the king of oils, so important that the olive was the symbol for the fourth letter of an early ancient alphabet.

Egyptian drawings of about 1000 BC depict olive trees, and the olive was placed alongside garlic and wine in tombs to provide sustenance in the hereafter. Olive oil was also mixed with the material for the mummy's wrap after which, the mummy was adorned with an olive branch. Yet, much of the olive oil in ancient Egypt was imported from Syria, leading scholars to believe that Egyptian olives produced inferior oils. Only during Roman domination was a small area in Egypt ever truly recognized for olives. Nevertheless, cured olives are believed to have been important to the ancient Egyptian diet.

Olive cultivation ultimately spread west through North Africa and to southern Europe. Its oil soon became an important trading commodity throughout the ancient Mediterranean.

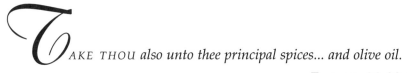

ᴛᴀᴋᴇ ᴛʜᴏᴜ also unto thee principal spices... and olive oil.

—Exodus 30:22-33

ᴛʜᴇ Oʟᴅ Tᴇsᴛᴀᴍᴇɴᴛ is filled with references to the olive and its oil. Two of the most important references are in Genesis and in Judges: in the former, a dove holding an olive branch in its mouth as a peace offering visits Noah with the message that the waters had receded; in the latter, the olive is appointed king of trees "...and they said unto the olive tree, reign thou over us."

The olive was often connected to the spiritual and material wealth of ancient Hebrew societies. The wealthy King David chose his most trusted men to act as supervisors over the prized olive, and King Solomon's tabernacle was made of what was considered sacred olive wood. But no ritual was more important to the Jews than to anoint the kings of Israel, and Moses was told to do so with a preparation of olive oil and spices.

The practice of ritual oil anointing was carried over from Judaism into Christianity. And it is no accident that the city of Jerusalem was founded at the foot of the Mount of Olives, and that Jesus, the Anointed One, spent his last days in and around the site, at the Garden of Gethsemane, derived from the Hebrew *gath-semen*, which means *oil press*.

Quite popular in the Middle East, the following seafood dish makes great use of the olive.

INGREDIENTS TO SERVE AS APPETIZER FOR A GROUP
2 cloves garlic, crushed
1 lb. mackerel
3 tbl. olive oil
2 onions, sliced

2 green peppers, sliced
1 lb. tomatoes, skinned and chopped
1 tbl. tomato paste
1 dozen pitted black olives
1 cup of parsley, chopped
crushed black pepper to taste

Scale and clean the fish, fry in olive oil on medium heat until lightly cooked. Remove and reserve on a platter; keep the oil hot.

Fry the onions in the oil until they are translucent, then add the green pepper and fry until they are soft and sweet. Add the garlic and fry one-minute more. Add the tomatoes, tomato paste, parsley and half cup of water, plus black pepper to taste, stir, bring to a boil and simmer for ten minutes.

Add the fish, being sure it is completely covered with the sauce, and cook for ten to fifteen minutes, adding a little water to keep it from drying. Add the olives at the last minute.

Arrange the fish on a serving platter and pour the sauce over it; chill and serve cold.

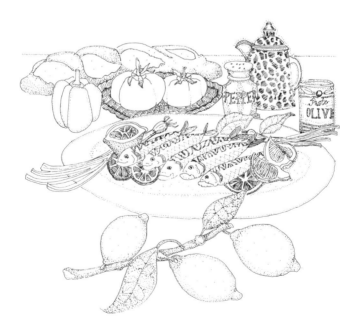

SAMOS AND MINOAN TRADE ROUTE

*T*HE TINY GREEK ISLAND OF SAMOS was important to the ancient Minoan olive-trading sea route with the Greek mainland. The name, Samos, loosely means, *planted in olives.* As you approach the island today in the small commuter plane that gets you there from Athens, thousands of olive trees are in plain view. On a usual day, the trees expose the rich silver-gray underbelly of their tiny oval-shaped leaves. But during hotter weather, the deep green topside of the leaves shimmer in the bright, almost constant, Samos sunshine. If the leaves are curled slightly you know the island suffers a particularly dry period.

Samos is an insular place, an ancient, quiet village island in the Aegean. Farming and fishing are its resources. Small islands like Samos come without the bustling city traffic and glittering nightlife. The locals make their own entertainment.

On our first day on the island Anne and I had lunch at a small restaurant in the center of the village-square. As far as we could tell, we were the only English-speaking foreigners—perhaps the only foreigners—visiting the island at the time. The custom in Greek restaurants is to pick your meal not off a menu but directly from the proprietor's counter, inside of which you find the day's offerings displayed. We spoke hardly any Greek, but to pick our meals all we did was to point.

As soon as we sat down to lunch a short, wiry, dark Greek came over to our table and in Australian English introduced himself as Peter. He said he was raised on Samos but had been living in Australia for many years. He was home for a visit and missed speaking English. When he discovered we had rented a car, Peter offered to take us on a tour, which, it turned out, included all the tavernas on the island.

Peter explained that at each stop he would first introduce us to his old cronies and then we would have to engage in the welcoming custom of downing a shot of ouzo. Not wanting to appear antisocial by refusing to engage in the local custom, we did what Peter suggested—ouzo is a liqueur flavored with anise, similar to Italian anisette; it is 40 percent alcohol.

Anne was the only woman in the tavernas but she kept up with everyone in the ouzo department, a fact that did not go unnoticed by the Greek men. After we dropped Peter off at his mother's home, having made a friend of every man in every taverna on Samos, we returned to our hotel and fell into a deep, deep sleep.

The following day we decided to soberly explore the island on our own. We traced our tracks from the previous day to a pretty beach. Octopus, calamari and sponge are big sea crops in the Aegean. As we walked the beach, gazing at the clear sea—we could see fish swimming underwater—we came upon a fisherman who was pounding octopus on some rocks, which was how the locals cleaned and tenderized them.

By mid-morning, unusual rain clouds burst overhead. To escape the staggering deluge, we ran for shelter to a nearby taverna. It wasn't quite lunchtime but after two ouzos (we had gotten the habit) we decided to put food into our stomachs.

With the chef behind the counter grinning and a waiter standing off to the side, offering a friendly guided point to what he believed would have suited our appetite, we pointed to the glisteningly white calamari that spread in a row under glass and over ice. The taverna was within yards of the Aegean, and that is where the calamari we selected had been residing just a few minutes earlier.

The rain was still beating down on Samos when we finished what turned out to be the most delightfully memorable meal of our visit to Greece, not to mention one of the best uses of olive oil in creation. By then it was truly lunch hour and the taverna filled with the loud island laborers who knocked back their ouzo and settled in for the three-hour mid-day meal. The chef, who was also the owner, was ecstatic when we decided to stay, and when we asked for a second round of the same lunch, he served it himself, with a free glass of wine. Of course the perfect accompaniment with the calamari dish was a dry, Samian house white wine.

INGREDIENTS TO SERVE TWO
3 cloves garlic, chopped
2 ounces olive oil
cayenne to taste
about six large calamari
¼ cup flour
1 egg
lemon
chopped parsley

Clean the squid: cut the tentacles from the head and put aside, then cut the heads off and throw them out. With this task accomplished, you will have cleaned away the black ink pockets located near the eyes and you will have isolated another edible portion of the squid—its tentacles. Slit the squid at the stomach, to open and flatten it. Take out the stuff inside, which includes a thin bone that you'd swear is made of plastic.

You must par-boil the squid to keep it from curling up in the pan when you sauté it. Fill a steamer pot with water and bring it to a boil. Put the squid bodies into the strainer portion of the steamer then dip the strainer into the boiling water for just a few seconds and remove the squid. (Sometimes you can find squid steaks on the market, cut from truly large squid. They can be used for this dish and they do not have to be par-boiled first. You need only one steak for each diner.)

Mix with a fork the egg and a squirt of lemon. Lay out the flour on a flat surface.

Mix each squid, individually, in the egg batter, let drain, and then roll each side in the flour. Do the same with the tentacles; then, repeat the procedure.

Add olive oil to a large pan. Add garlic to the pan and cook at medium heat for one minute. Sprinkle the pan with cayenne to taste.

Add the squid to the pan and cook until the batter is golden on each side (1 to 2 minutes per side). Serve with a lemon wedge and parsley garnish.

Properly cooked squid is slightly crunchy and ever full of the smell and taste of the sea.

*A*S THEY DO WITH WINE, Asian cultures show minimal interest in olive oil, and this is understandable. Asians enjoy wonderful sources of oil from the ancient nuts and seeds that flourish in the East, and some say the delicate Asian cooking could well be interrupted by the forward taste of olive oil. Still, China is said to grow four times as many olive trees as France, but the reason is unclear.

The peanut became the primary source for cooking oil in Asia and parts of Africa after its introduction from the New World during the Age of Discovery. Today, India produces about one third of the world's peanut crops, followed by China and the United States, and the peanut is an important export crop of West Africa.

During research for this book I discovered a curious parallel among major peanut producing countries: India, China and West Africa combined produce no note-worthy quantity of wine relative to populations, and each enjoy hardly any per-capita wine consumption; the United States is fourth in world wine production, but it has the lowest per-capita consumption of the top ten industrial nations, and it ranks 36 in the top 66 wine-consuming nations.

The lack of olive oil notwithstanding, Indian and Chinese recipes that make use of garlic, nut oils and nuts are delightful and they pair beautifully with either fruity or dessert wines.

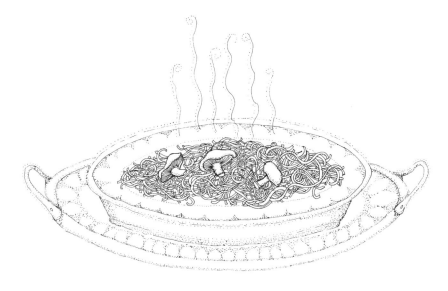

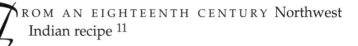ROM AN EIGHTEENTH CENTURY Northwest Indian recipe [11]

INGREDIENTS
1 bulb of garlic, pressed
½ cup of oil (peanut)
½ pound cubed mutton
sweet herbs
(nutmeg, mace, coriander, cumin sweetened with sugar)
salt and pepper

Stuff the meat with the sweet herbs and skewer, putting more sweet herbs between each slice of meat. Dip in crushed garlic and oil, then salt and pepper to taste.

Roast on a spit, continually basting with the oil and garlic.

Cook until done the way you like your meat.

*B*UT THEN, perhaps the olive oil grown in China does have a cooking purpose...

INGREDIENTS TO SERVE TWO
4 cloves garlic, chopped
2 tbl. olive oil
1 tbl. sesame oil
½ cup fruity white wine or sherry
handful of unsalted, roasted cashews
1 leek, chopped
1 sweet red pepper, sliced
1 cup of broccoli tips
½ pound chicken breast bits or sliced pork
1 tbl. chopped basil leaves
3 tbl. powdered curry mix (you can add extra ginger if you prefer)
1 hot Thai red pepper, chopped (or other hot pepper)
¼ cup heavy cream

Add leek, sweet pepper and broccoli tips to olive oil in a wok over medium heat. Cook for five minutes, stirring constantly.

Add garlic, ¼ cup wine, basil, 1 tbl. curry (and extra ginger) and hot pepper to the wok and stir. Cook for ten minutes.

Throw in the meat and add sesame oil; add another ¼ cup of wine and stir vigorously for the next five to seven minutes, adding a dash of water if the liquid dries up.

Just before serving, lower the flame, add the cashews, the rest of the curry and pour a circle of heavy cream into the wok. Stir and mix vigorously for a minute, turn off the flame and serve, over white rice if you prefer.

PART II

Classical Greece and Rome

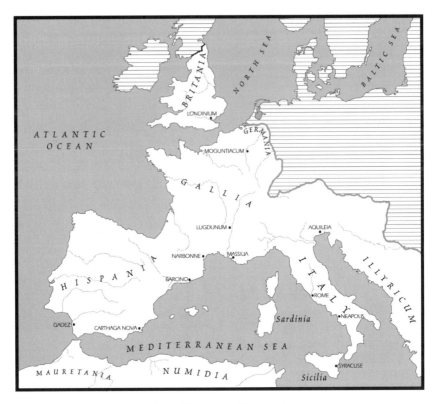

THE ROMAN EMPIRE

Garlic, Wine and Olive Oil

—4—

Garlic in the Mediterranean and Beyond

OW BOLT DOWN these cloves of garlic... you will have greater mettle for the fight.

—ARISTOPHANES' *KNIGHTS* [1]

HE PHOENICIANS traveled west into Mediterranean regions and into Europe where they established thriving economic communities at least ten centuries before the birth of Christ. Greek culture spread into the same Mediterranean regions soon after. In the third century BC Athenians introduced the finger-food cart: the cook offered a tray with five plates on it: a plate of garlic, three separate plates of seafood and one plate with a goblet of wine. This was a period of high Greek culture, and such times are often expressed in the menu. By this time, the Greeks had already established a pattern of three square meals a day, the upper class ate at least three courses for lunch and for supper, each with a reasonable dose of garlic.

Garlic played an important role in Greece's magic and mythology too. It was placed at crossroads as an offering to Hecate, the goddess of witchcraft and sorcery. In Homer's *Odyssey*, the hero escapes being changed into a pig by the virtues of moly, believed to be a wild species of Allium, and a magical protective given to him by the messenger god Hermes/Mercury.

Greek warriors took garlic for strength before a battle, as religiously as Greek midwives took an ample supply of garlic with them to ward off the Evil Eye when they delivered a baby. Like the ruling class and priests of many ancient cultures, the Greek upper class initially disdained superstitions connected to garlic, fearing that such beliefs had the power to sway the populace. But this attitude toward garlic had no place in medicine.

Hippocrates lived between the fourth and third centuries BC and is known as The Father of Medicine. He used garlic in his practice to treat cuts, infections, and gastro-intestinal disease. In the next century, during the time of Aristotle, the first to assign scientific categories to plants, Theophrastus, documented the importance of garlic as an agricultural crop.

During the first century AD, Dioscorides created a widely distributed pharmacopoeia of medicinal preparations. In his "Herbal of Dioscorides" the Greek physician claimed garlic preparations cured ailments from tapeworm, to bed bug bites, to the bite of a shrew. According to Lloyd Harris (*The Book of Garlic*), many of Dioscorides' pharmacological preparations outlived the Western Roman Empire and were brought to the Byzantine Court at Constantinople. From there the preparations survived Islam and the Ottoman Empire and were still in use in early nineteenth-century Turkey.

Many Greek physicians and scientists lived under Roman rule, and yet some scholars believe that Roman aristocrats disdained garlic. In a fourth century AD aristocratic gourmet cookbook by Apicius, *De Re Coquinara* (Of Things Culinary), no recipes included garlic. For seasoning, Romans often used the already-mentioned, extremely pungent asafoetida instead.

MEAT SAUCE FOR NINE,
the customary number of people at a Roman
dinner party in the 1st century AD. [2]

INGREDIENTS
¼ ounce each of asafoetida, caraway, celery seed, cumin, cyperus,
dill, ginger, hazelwort, lovage, parsley and pepper
some pyrethrum (chrysanthemum)
1¼ pints garum (a strong, liquid sauce made mostly of fermented
fish, salt and wine, and aged for months; sometimes
referred to as liquamen)
2½ ounces olive oil

*W*E SHALL NOT BE SURPRISED TOO, *that it (garlic) acts as a powerful remedy for the bite of a shrew...*

—*NATURAL HISTORY*, PLINY, 1ST CENTURY AD [3]

*N*OTWITHSTANDING aristocratic fears of garlic, from Virgil to Pliny, Roman writers listed scores of beneficial uses for it. Pliny listed 61 garlic remedies in his *Natural History*, including remedies for hemorrhoids, bruises, skin ulcerations, blisters, asthma, dropsy, jaundice, toothache, earache, catarrh, hoarseness, coughs, intestinal parasites and the bite of a shrew that the Greek, Dioscorides, mentioned. Pliny also recommended an aphrodisiac of garlic and coriander taken in wine.

Although laws were passed prohibiting those who entered Roman temples from having garlic breath—that age-old fear of its powers to sway the public—the revered second century AD physician, Galen, made it clear to Roman Emperors that garlic had both healing and nutritional powers. Galen called garlic "Theriaca Rusticoriam" (Poor Man's Treacle) and due, in part to the physician's teachings, the Roman government decreed that soldiers and laborers regularly be fed garlic to foster strength and endurance, especially while marauding or working the land in extremely hot temperatures.

*I*N THE SECOND CENTURY *of the Christian era, the Empire of Rome comprehended the fairest part of the earth, and the most civilized portion of mankind.*

—EDWARD GIBBON, *DECLINE AND FALL OF THE ROMAN EMPIRE* [4]

*T*HE ROMAN EMPIRE converted the entire Mediterranean region, plus north and northeastern Europe into efficient, productive agricultural trading colonies. Methods of food transportation and storage were refined, new understanding in science and medicine developed and technology created such practical wonders as the efficient vertical mill wheel and the invention of the screw press.

By the time it reached its end in the sixth century, the Western Roman Empire had done more to spread agricultural and scientific advancements than any earlier dominant culture. But after the fall of Rome, as the agriculturally productive Roman provinces scattered into many small warring kingdoms, barbarians and anarchy swept the Italic peninsula and major parts of northern Europe. The new Byzantine Empire emerged in Turkey where it became a Christian stronghold.

Trade among the western Roman provinces all but disappeared. Inexpensive aromatic plants like leeks, onion and garlic took on major importance to replace the more expensive spices of the East, which were now difficult to get. Most meals were prepared from what peasants could harvest in their backyards.

In the sixth century a Roman aristocrat, Cassiodorus, served the Goths in what is now northern Italy. When the Byzantine Empire re-captured the territory, afraid because of his aristocratic western Roman roots, Cassiodorus fled south where he established a hermitage and monastery that became crucial to the preservation of Latin literature and scientific writings, much the same way the priests of ancient Mesopotamia guarded over early literature. Cassiodorus' monastery in Squillace was the catalyst for the practice of copying manuscripts that flourished in monasteries throughout Europe in the Middle Ages. The scant culinary and medicinal writings that do exist for the period between the 8th and 13th centuries

Garlic, Wine and Olive Oil

were preserved in the libraries of those monasteries.

Monks became the gardeners and physicians of the period. They helped to expand garlic cultivation throughout Europe, thereby making it plentiful and cheap. Medieval physician monks treated lepers—known as pilgarlics—by administering raw garlic cloves. The monks also treated bald men, also known as pilgarlics, by macerating 4 garlic bulbs in a quart of clear spirits, and then massaging it into the scalp before shampooing. (This is the one garlic recipe that personal experience proves does not work.)

Even in tenth century Byzantium eastern spices were hard to come by. A most popular dish at the Imperial Court was roast goat stuffed with garlic, leeks and onions smothered in a sauce similar to the Roman liquamen or garum described by Apicius.

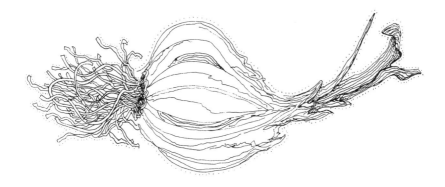

*T*HIS IS TO BE UNDERSTOOD *of healthy eyes, but those which are dull through vicious humidity, from these garlic drives this viciousness away.*
—HEALING LORE IN A MONASTERY [5]

*G*ARLIC'S PRESERVATIVE PROPERTIES were especially important during the medieval period of poor sanitary conditions and no refrigeration. So in spite of a renewed disdain of kings, queens and the aristocracy, garlic use prevailed in all of medieval Europe, and England especially remained a major garlic-eating country. Garlic remained an important crop as well in Eastern Europe and in parts of Asia; in Siberia you could pay your taxes to the state with 15 bulbs of garlic for each man.

As medieval monks copied and recopied Greek, Roman and Arab literature with the help of garlic to drive "vicious humidity" from their eyes, they also transcribed herbal and medicinal treatises, many of which formed the basis for English herbalists of the period of the Renaissance. One of the well-known herbalists, John Gerard, believed that garlic heated the body, was an enemy to cold poisons and to venomous bites, soothed a rough throat and killed worms in the belly, all of which echoed the ancients like Sus'Ruta, Pliny, Hippocrates, Dioscorides and Galen. Other English herbalists and botanists of the period shared Gerard's garlic sentiments.

14TH CENTURY RECIPE FOR SAUCE [6]

Take flour and cow's milk, ground saffron, garlic and put into a fair little pot; and seethe it over the fire, and serve it forth.

*E*AT NO ONIONS, *nor garlic, for we are to utter sweet breath...*
—WM. SHAKESPEARE, *A MIDSUMMER NIGHT'S DREAM*

Garlic, Wine and Olive Oil

*I*N SPITE OF THE PRAISE of English herbalists and physicians, other beliefs about garlic, that it represented the Devil, plus a dislike of its pungency, began to emerge in England at the dawn of the Age of Discovery.

Thanks to the invention of the printing press, many cookbooks appeared in Europe toward the end of the Middle Ages. In England, garlic was particularly absent from a great deal of the recipes, leading some scholars to believe that its appeal was in decline at the time. Certainly by the 17th century the British upper class entirely rejected garlic and British cooking reflected that fact. No doubt, extensive use of garlic in the colonial East confirmed its low standing with the British upper class. By the Victorian era, the British aristocracy allowed no place for garlic on its tables.

Garlic fared differently on the continent. When a boy was born to thirteenth century Jews of Barcelona, they slaughtered a rooster and hung its head, adorned with garlic, over the front door. In sixteenth-century France garlic was called "the camphor of the poor"—the lips of French newborns were anointed with it to stimulate and cleanse. During an eighteenth-century plague at Marseilles, thieves were said to have made profits by relieving the bodies of plague victims of their valuables. The thieves were believed immune to infection of the disease because of their heavy intake of garlic macerated in wine.

GREEK SEA ROUTE TO ITALIC PENINSULA

Garlic, Wine and Olive Oil

Wine in the Mediterranean and Beyond

*T*HE GREEKS LEARNED about wine in the Phoenician trading center of Thrace. By 1000 BC Greek culture had become the first to make wine readily available to the general populace as a basic daily food—making wine an even greater economic force than it had been in earlier civilizations.

Three thousand years ago family vineyards filled the Greek countryside; the farmers made wine mainly for personal consumption. In major Greek cultural city centers like Athens, the elite drank highly prized imported wines from the Greek islands. As Greece expanded its sphere of influence, its wines became the standard by which all wine was measured. It was heavy stuff, high in alcohol, rich to the taste and was usually cut with seawater, honey or herbs. It was often preserved in amphorae with an addition of pitch or pine resin—an idea the Greeks got from the Phoenicians. Modern filtration and clarification techniques create cleaner and more elegant wines that no longer require extensive additives or preservatives. Yet, the Greeks continue to produce a wine containing pine resin; it is called retsina and it tastes like undiluted turpentine. But I did not know this before the first time I tried it.

As in many Mediterranean coastal locales, the custom on the Greek island of Samos is to eat a late dinner. After dinner, a promenade along the shore is in order, which Anne and I did each of the four evenings we spent on the tiny island, except one. On this night, we had gone to the only restaurant in the vicinity of our *pensione* with the intention to order a glass each of retsina before dinner, just to find out what it was like. We had already been warned against trying to drink any more. The waiter misunderstood our order for two glasses, bringing instead two one-liter bottles, opened.

When faced with a potentially embarrassing and near impossible situation, Anne often displays more common sense than I do—this was one of those times. She tasted, and did not like retsina. She put her bottle aside and ordered a glass of table wine.

I tasted and disliked retsina too, but I could not let the rest of it go to waste, so I drank it, claiming it tasted better with each succeeding swallow. So as not to waste Anne's bottle of retsina, we gave it to some locals seated at a table nearby.

We finished our dinner and proceeded for our walk along the shore, in my case, on wobbly legs. But I did not make it more than fifteen feet from the restaurant before my stomach erupted in a pine resinous heave. It was not until the following day, at lunch, when I began to once again feel that life was preferable over death. That was more than twenty-five years ago—I have yet to drink another glass of retsina.

Garlic, Wine and Olive Oil

Illustration by Tina Howe

*E*QUALLY BLESSING THE RICH, *the poor, he has conferred the joy of wine.*

—EURIPIDES, *THE BACCHAE* 7A

OUR FIRST NIGHT IN ATHENS found Anne and me in a restaurant located just up the street from the Acropolis. Its elegant but simply prepared food, its wait staff and its location conspired to lure us back many times.

The restaurant's outdoor seating spanned two sides of the street. The waiters—they were always male—dodged traffic in order to get from the kitchen to the diners across the street. We sat at our sidewalk table, under the influence of the spectacular lights that flooded the great Acropolis, devouring the inexpensive, but marvelous dishes of stuffed grapevine leaves, eggplant and marinated octopus that our waiter, Nick, recommended.

Nick was a slender, dark young Greek who was particularly adept at getting to and from the kitchen—trays held high, cars be damned. He once lived in New York City, which is where, he said, he learned the most effective way to cross a busy street was to run.

Prevailing wisdom that the best white wines are produced in cooler climates does not follow in Greece. The best wines we tasted in Greece were white and they were produced either in relatively warm Athens or on the warm Aegean Greek islands. Our waiter, Nick, recommended wines we could not find back in the United States, one was a beautiful Athenian wine called Pallini, and it matched perfectly a dish Nick also recommended—stuffed grape leaves. Generally, however, the wines from the islands were superior, especially the wines of Rhodos and at its city named Lindos.

We had a memorable dinner our first night on the island of Rhodos, at an outdoor seafood restaurant. It was a simple yet satisfying meal of light consommé, a spinach-based vegetable dish and lobsters, made superb first by the way the Rhodos wine—followed by the Lindos wine—paired perfectly with the lobster, and second by the unbelievably inexpensive price tag to the evening: about $30. After dinner we took the customary promenade along the beach. As the moon rose over the Mediterranean, what was during daytime a placid bay had turned into a windy, tumultuous beachhead of great romantic force, and the wine and food we had taken at dinner fortified us to meet the gale head on.

Back in Athens, on our last night, Nick recommended cold stuffed grape leaves and the fruity Pallini wine to match.

Garlic, Wine and Olive Oil

40-50 fresh vine leaves, plus a few extra
3-4 cloves of garlic, sliced
½ cup olive oil
¾ cup long grain rice
2-3 tomatoes, skinned and chopped
1 large onion, chopped
2½ tbl. finely chopped parsley
2½ tbl. dried crushed mint
¼ tsp. each ground cinnamon and ground allspice
1 tsp. sugar
1 lemon
salt and pepper to taste
yogurt (optional)

Dip the vine leaves in boiling water until they are limp (a few minutes).

Stir the rice in boiling water for a few minutes and then rinse it in cold water; drain it completely and then mix the rice with tomatoes, onion, parsley, mint, cinnamon, allspice and salt and pepper to taste. This is the filling.

Place one leaf on a plate, vein side up. Put 1 tsp. of filling near the stem edge; then fold the stem end over the filling, fold each side toward the middle and roll closed. Squeeze the stuffed leaf lightly, put aside and do the next leaf until you have filled all of them.

Pack the leaves tightly in a pan lined with the extra grapevine leaves; slip a slice of garlic in between the leaves every now and again.

Mix the olive oil and a half cup of water, plus the sugar and juice of a lemon; pour the mixture over the stuffed leaves. Place a plate over the leaves to keep them from unrolling, cover the pan and simmer mildly for 2 hours, occasionally adding a cup of water to keep it moist.

Cool and then refrigerate and serve chilled, topped with plain yogurt.

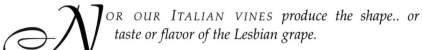

OR OUR ITALIAN VINES produce the shape.. or taste or flavor of the Lesbian grape.

—VIRGIL, ROMAN POET [8]

HE GREEKS landed on the southern Italic peninsula in about 1000 BC. They introduced and taught the local dairy farmers modern farming methods for grain, wine and olive oil. Within two centuries Greece had colonized the southern mainland and Sicily. Greek food, wine and thought made an impact from Sicily to the shores of the Tiber River; north of the Tiber was under the care of the industrious Etruscans.

Like the Greeks, Etruscan culture included wine—their mythological wine god, with the incredible name Flufluns, descended from the same mother of the Greek wine god, Dionysus, who was later called Bacchus by the Romans. Perhaps Etruscans, who seemed to drink wine mainly for its effect were not as sophisticated as the Greeks, who mostly revered wine as a food.

In the fifth century BC, a small northwest-central village of dairy farmers expelled the Etruscan king, Tarquin, to make room for the new Republic of Rome. Rome knew the Etruscans as the creators of the "Bacchanalia"—a practiced ritual with an established reputation for debauchery and licentiousness, not to mention human sacrifice. Romans viewed Etruscan women as loose and the men as drunkards, and worse, the Etruscans engaged in ritual superstitions. The early Roman Republic lived for a time in guarded tolerance of its wine-consuming northern neighbors.

As did southerners on the peninsula, Roman shepherds consumed a heavy dairy diet. During the early stages of the Republic, one of its mythical founders, Romulus, is even said to have made the libation to the gods with milk, and early republican law prohibited women, and men under thirty, from consuming wine. Rome might have been influenced some by Etruria, but the Republic was greatly influenced by its relationship with and finally its conquest of Greece and assimilation of Greek culture.

Garlic, Wine and Olive Oil

*L*IKE THE GREEKS, commoners in the Roman Republic practiced subsistence farming. Greece's best wines, however, continued to fill the stomachs of the Roman aristocracy. But in the second century BC the Roman Senator, Cato, the Elder, published De Agri Cultura (Of Things Agricultural). The treatise was a boon to Roman viticulture; it spelled out in detail how to propagate, plant, cultivate and sell grapes and wine. Cato even made recommendations on how to treat the vineyard labor force.

Following Cato by three centuries, a renowned agronomist, Columella, brought efficiency to Roman vineyards. Columella developed large capitalist viticultural practices, some of which are still in use throughout the world today. Following Columella's advice, profitable industrial farming contracts replaced the family farm in Rome. But even the shrewd Columella once wrote that the whole of Mediterranean viticulture owed a debt to Carthage—he was referring to a book written by a Carthaginian named Mago.

The Carthaginians were descendants of the Phoenicians so they knew something about wine. Mago's book got into Roman hands during the Punic Wars and Rome's merciless sacking of Carthage in 146 BC. The book detailed vine propagation, vineyard planting and care, determining grape quality, marketing grapes for wine and vineyard slave labor distribution, and seems to have been the source for Cato's instructions.

New viticultural practices in Rome led to the most famous ancient vintage in literature: the vintage of 121 BC. That year the spectacular wines of the southern region of Campania reached their zenith. One of the most sought-after wines of the period, Falernian, was produced on a small hill in Campania for the next few centuries. Over time, however, Falernian's owners succumbed to the great demand for its wine and the great promise of profits by cutting costs and reducing care. By the first century AD, it had become a mass-produced wine of inferior quality living off its reputation.

The fact that there was so much wine, and that it had become one of the daily basic requirements, gave the Roman government an excuse to impose taxes on seemingly wealthy wine producers. Often the taxes were paid in wine instead of cash, and much of the wine was then distributed in a welfare program to the general public. A lot of the wine collected by the government also went with Roman legions as they conquered Europe and North Africa.

The great Campanian vintage of 121 BC spelled the beginning of the end for Greek wine dominance, and as Rome became an empire, many of the newly established provinces excelled at wine production.

Although Roman and Greek physicians used it freely as a base for medicinal elixirs, wine was primarily a Roman food; its quality was an important subject. Laws and regulations were established to ensure quality and proper distribution. The Romans also discovered the aging potential of wine. Their practice of heating wines at the top level of the "smoke house" was precursor to pasteurization which both stabilized wine by killing off potential spoilage organisms and gave sophistication to its flavor by speeding up the aging process.

Roman appreciation of individual wines with certain foods, led to many traditional local wine and food dishes like the following.

OLD SOUTHERN ROMAN RECIPE FOR LAMB [9]

INGREDIENTS
lamb
olive oil
garlic
egg yolks
lemon peel
dry white wine

Cut the lamb into 1 inch chunks. Mix all the ingredients into a frying pan and cook until done to your taste.

According to Waverly Root (*The Food of Italy*), the Romans likely paired the above with a refreshingly acidic Frascati, or perhaps they were partial to a dry red produced farther south in the Lazio region, near the border with Campania.

OLD UMBRIAN RECIPE FOR SPAGHETTI [10]

INGREDIENTS
spaghetti
garlic
olive oil
ginger
parsley

Cook garlic and ginger in olive oil and mix in cooked spaghetti, serve with parsley garnish.

A glass of semi-dry white Orvieto from north of Rome was likely the wine for this dish.

I WONDER OFTEN *what the vintners buy*
One half so precious as the goods they sell...
— THE RUBAIYAT OF OMAR KHAYYAM [11]

VITICULTURE AND WINEMAKING were the main activities at the monastery of the fourth century Coptic monk, Hilarion, in Gaza. Fifth and sixth century Christians in the fallen western provinces of the Roman Empire made pilgrimages to Gaza and to Jerusalem, which had become the Christian Holy Land. The pilgrims brought wine back to their homeland, and when the quality of the wine was recognized, old eastern Mediterranean trade routes once again were well traversed. Greece, Turkey, Syria and all of Palestine were restored to their ancient role as center for the wine trade.

Between the fourth and sixth centuries the hills near Aleppo in northern Syria were major sources of wine exports to Antioch and Apamea, important cities in the Byzantine Empire. Seventh century invasions by Persians, and later Arab invasions, threatened trade between the Middle East and Turkey. Soon the rebirth of the vast ancient eastern Mediterranean wine trade had been halted for good.

Early Moslem zealots destroyed vineyards as they expanded into Europe and the Mediterranean. Yet, it is difficult to reconcile the Moslem anti-wine sentiment with the course of Moslem societies. In tenth-century Spain the Moors refined the already known process for distilling grape brandy—a good wine is the base for a good brandy. And there are the many glowing references to wine found in numerous writings of Islamic poets like Khayyam and Hafiz. But the most interesting paradox relating to the relationship between wine and Moslems is that while the Islamic holy book, the Koran, discourages its use, and modern Moslem societies ban it, wine enjoys three separate positive references in the Koran, including this promise to the pious: "This is the paradise which the righteous have been promised. There shall flow in it rivers of unpolluted water, and rivers of milk forever fresh; rivers of delectable wine

Garlic, Wine and Olive Oil

and rivers of clearest honey..." (Sura XLVII. 15).

It is also interesting that in the most recent available figures (1997) Iran ranked sixth in world vineyard acreage, more than either Germany, Portugal, Greece, Argentina, Chile, Hungary or Australia. As to the use for its 667,000 acres, we are left to speculate.

While Moslem expansionists burned vineyards, medieval Christian monks in northern Europe and parts of the Mediterranean persuaded peasants to give their vineyards to the monasteries and to work in their self-contained communities. To both save their souls and to keep their land productive, many in the wealthy class did the same. By the ninth century, after Charlemagne had stabilized Germany and parts of eastern Europe, he gave extensive vineyard properties to monasteries. Many of those monasteries became famous for their wines, often using the wine as a means to keep valuable community members from straying and to keep barbarians at bay. Some of the great German and Hungarian wine-producing houses today are direct descendants of monasteries and nunneries that flourished under Charlemagne. The same situation took place in most of northern France, where the famous medieval monastery at Saint-Germain-des-Pres, in Paris, produced about 11,000 gallons of wine each year. Important monasteries in Burgundy and Champagne that began during this period flourished well into the seventeenth century.

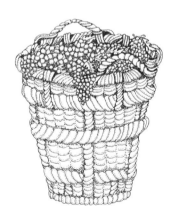

E CARE NOT FOR MONEY, riches, or wealth
Old sack (sherry) is our money, old sack is our wealth...
—THOMAS RANDOLPH, ENGLISH POET [12]

OWARD THE LATTER PART OF THE MIDDLE AGES southern European wines had fallen out of favor. The interest shifted to wine districts in the north and in eastern European countries that managed to hold off Islamic rule. Hungary, Germany, northern France, northern Italy and northern Spain produced the best wines. Milan, Bruges, Koln, London and Champagne became major trade centers—the latter had been the site of the most important annual trade fair between the thirteenth and fourteenth centuries.

A growing wine trade meant the expansion of vineyards. Many of the popular Vitis vinifera grape varieties we know today were introduced into northern Europe during this period: Trebbiano, Cabernet Franc and Pinot Noir, for instance. Pinot Noir is arguably the most revered red wine grape, and because of its temperamental personality on the vine, wine made from this grape is difficult to produce. Pinot Noir is represented at the oldest, most well known annual wine auction in the world today, at the Hospice de Beaune, in Burgundy's capital city.

The hospice, which provided medical care for the poor, was formed in the mid-fifteenth century by a rogue tax collector named Nicolas Rolin. As Chancellor of the Duchy of Burgundy during Louis XI's reign, Rolin's sticky palms made him a rich man. He also had a flair for public relations, a trait that helped to keep him safe from the monarch and, at least in one instance, helped to soothe his conscience.

Rolin persuaded landowners in Beaune to make gifts of vineyards to the hospice. The vineyard holdings swelled quickly so Rolin came up with the concept of an annual wine auction from the many vineyards to help pay the hospice's bills.

Today, the annual November wine auction at the Hospice de

Garlic, Wine and Olive Oil

Beaune is a barometer for the quality of past and future vintages in the region.

Under Roman rule, England had produced a small amount of wine, but by the Middle Ages most British vineyards had vanished, either by neglect or because of devastating wars with France. Yet the British thirst for wine seemed unquenchable, and England became the largest importer of wine. Britain's interests in western France, its ties with Dutch and German exporters and its merchant trade with Spain and Portugal, provided the British people with some of the best wines in the world: claret from Bordeaux, port and Madeira from Portugal, Rhenish from Germany and sherry (sack) from Spain.

ANCIENT MARINATED-OLIVE APPETIZER

Heat chopped garlic with wine vinegar thoroughly in a pan. Chill and then pour over olives and marinate for twenty-four hours. Before serving, add olive oil and stir the mixture.

—6—

Olives in the Mediterranean and Beyond

HE OLIVE TREE extracts nutrition from the soil, but offers little to the soil in return. Some historians claim this particular feature of the tree was instrumental in turning the land around Athens into a dry, barren desert. After being introduced to the olive about 3,000 years ago, the Greeks spread the cultivation of its trees and curing of its fruit throughout the Mediterranean. In the sixth century BC the Athens legislator, Solon, decreed that the olive would be the only crop exported from the great city. The decision later proved disastrous to the Greek economy, yet Solon might have had little choice in the matter.

A close reading of history shows that economics and the need to feed growing populations was a driving force behind expansionism and colonization. As the strength of Rome developed, it of course encroached on Greek economic and agricultural interests. The sacking of Carthage gave Rome a dominant position in Mediterranean grain production. Greece, which had strong trading interests in the southern mainland of the Italic peninsula, in Sicily and in Carthage in North Africa, had already abandoned its once powerful grain markets. Because Carthage grain production was massive and cheaper, Roman grain farmers lost their markets too—following Cato's advice, many of them turned to vineyards. Grapevines grew in importance, and after the marvelous vintage of 121 BC, and with continuing Roman expansion, Rome ultimately overcame the Greek wine trade.

For a time Greece's reliance on the economic strength of the olive held. But as Rome's economic and military power grew, the glory of Classical Greece could not be held up by one crop. Luckily, before Greece faded, its culture had made a lasting imprint on the southern and eastern Mediterranean regions, and on Rome.

*T*O THE CLASSICAL GREEK and to Roman aristocrats butter was food for barbarians. In Rome bread was eaten dry or it was dipped in milk or wine—sometimes for breakfast. Dipping bread in olive oil, which modern-day Tuscans do with love in their eyes, is a recently established ritual.

Romans either ate the olive whole or used its oil for cooking. Olive oil was also used extensively in Rome as a weed killer, insect repellent on vegetables, as axle grease for chariots and to grease up athletes; and scrapings of olive oil and sweat from recognized athletes was sold to mix in medicines!

In Imperial Rome olive oil production burgeoned and its trade was highly organized. The olive oil exchange "arca olearia" created a bustling private Roman oil trade of imports and exports. Like their vineyard plantings, Romans spread olive plantings extensively, as far north as the foothills of the Alps. And as it was with wine, Campania was considered one of the best olive oil producing areas of the second century BC. But olive oil was in such demand that Rome also imported a great deal of it from Iberia, North Africa and Greece. The top olive-producing countries today are all in the Mediterranean region, and all were once part of the Roman Empire: Spain, Italy, Greece and much of the Middle East and North Africa.

The Romans cured and ate many types of olives, from unripe to over ripe. Two favorite recipes were a salad of pitted olives cured in oil and spices, eaten with cheese and an olive cake made from pressed pulp of olive, salted and flavored with spices.

In addition to writing about wine and viticulture, Cato wrote about olive oil. He claimed that small, early picked, immature olives made the finest oil (the virgin oil) and that this best oil came from the first, delicate and cool pressing, which was made a lot easier by the Roman invention of the screw press. He also claimed

Garlic, Wine and Olive Oil

that when they were allowed to heat, picked olives fermented and the oil became rancid. To Cato, olive oil quality decreased with each subsequent pressing, and olives grown in hotter climates produced limpid, tasteless oil.

If he could visit Italy today Cato would be shocked to learn that Italians dip their bread in olive oil, but in olive oil production he would discover few surprises. The difference in production between the second century and this century is mainly in more modern presses and the use of the centrifuge to separate water from the oil—the old way was to rest and settle the oil.

With apologies to Cato and to other ancient Roman aristocrats, the following is one sure way to enjoy olive oil and bread combined:

INGREDIENTS
One loaf of freshly-baked light, airy bread with a crisp crust
4 to 6 garlic cloves, pressed
½ cup cold-pressed, extra virgin olive oil
a few basil leaves and a few mint leaves, chopped
black peppercorns, crushed

Add garlic, basil and peppercorns to the olive oil in a dipping bowl, and let sit at room temperature for at least 12 hours.

Break a piece of bread from the loaf and dip it in the olive oil; continue to do so until the bread is gone, or get more bread and dip until the olive oil is gone.

The above is a perfect way to start a meal or to snack.

Thomas Pellechia

*A*LLAH IS THE LIGHT *of the heavens and earth, and His light is as a lamp... The lamp is kindled from a blessed tree, an olive of neither East nor West... It is a light upon a light...*

—THE KORAN, SURA 24 [13]

Garlic, Wine and Olive Oil

*O*LIVE OIL PRODUCTION continued throughout the turmoil of the Dark and early Middle Ages, even though the extensive trade system the Romans established had collapsed. Certainly olive oil sometimes could have served a dubious purpose—to light torches for use during night raids, or to burn heretics at the stake—but the oil was mainly used to anoint those at the top of the religious hierarchy during a time of uncompromising religious fervor.

Christian monasteries in the northern Mediterranean, and those that survived Islamic domination of the southern and eastern Mediterranean, traded their olive oil in Europe's north where heating oil was in great demand and where the oil was used to make soap, cosmetics and as a lubricant. And since the olive tree was prevalent in the Levant, Moslems took seriously their stewardship over its valuable oil. About this time, appetizers of pitted olives became popular in some Islamic countries and the olive began to become a major source of calories for Moslems.

RECIPE FROM 13ᵀᴴ CENTURY IRAQ [14]

INGREDIENTS
black olives
salt, to taste
garlic
thyme
walnuts
sesame seeds and sesame oil

Pit, crush and salt the olives and leave them to rest, turning them over every day until their bitterness dissipates, then place them on a tray of woven sticks for at least 24 hours, or until they dry.

Pound garlic, dry thyme and walnuts, and put the mixture over a low fire, and put the olives in an oven underneath the fire and leave for a day, stirring periodically.

Serve seasoned with sesame oil, crushed walnuts, toasted sesame seeds, garlic and thyme.

PART III

Age of Discovery to Nineteenth Century

Garlic, Wine and Olive Oil

–7–

Garlic, Wine and Olives
Across the Pond

E ABSOLUTELY FORBID IT entrance into our salleting (salads), by reason of its intolerable rankness...

—JOHN EVELYN, 17TH-CENTURY,
INVENTOR OF THE SALAD IN AMERICA [1]

IFTEENTH AND SIXTEENTH CENTURY Spanish and Portuguese sailors introduced garlic to parts of South and North America, as potent folklore and as medicine; in Cuba it was believed that by hanging thirteen garlic cloves on a cord and then wearing it around your neck for thirteen days you could prevent jaundice; in the Andes explorers fought off mountain sickness by either sniffing or eating garlic.

Native American Indian medicine, which often included garlic, many times saved the intrepid but hopelessly ignorant European explorers from illness and starvation. Nevertheless, to the original British colonies of the Northeast and Southeast, many of whose revolutionary fathers descended from the British aristocracy, garlic was kept at arms distance. At the turn of the eighteenth century, garlic was not so revered in the hotbed of the British and American Enlightenment. In the early nineteenth century, heresy, legends and rumors disparaging garlic were rampant in the eastern part of the United States. Harris *(The Book of Garlic)* recounts the tales of a strange native tribe of garlic eaters, with large garlic bulbs for heads, located in Mexico, and of a particularly bizarre legend about a giant garlic of the Southwest that caused head-on train collisions and delayed railroad lines being built at the time.

Garlic simply was unimportant to the rugged North Americans whose diet was heavy in game meats, with recipes such as the one for opossum.

ROAST OPOSSUM: AN EARLY AMERICAN RECIPE [2]

TO MAKE THE STUFFING
1 large onion
1 tablespoon fat
opossum liver, finely chopped
1 cup bread crumbs
chopped sweet red pepper
dash of Worcestershire
1 hard boiled egg, chopped
salt

Brown the onion in fat. Add the liver and cook until tender. Add the crumbs, a red pepper, Worcestershire, egg, salt and water to moisten.

TO ROAST THE OPOSSUM

Dress the animal as you would a suckling pig, removing the entrails, head and tail. Wash thoroughly with steaming hot water. Cover with cold water and a cup of salt; let stand overnight.

Drain the salted water. Rinse well using clear boiling water; and then stuff the opossum and sew it closed. Place in a roasting pan, add 2 tbl. water to the pan and roast at 350 degrees for 1½ hours. Baste every 15 minutes with drippings.

Remove stitches and place on a heated platter. Skim the fat from the gravy in the pan.

Garlic, Wine and Olive Oil

To the British colonizer in the Age of Discovery, garlic was fit only for the colonized, a situation that lasted well into Victoria's reign. But after the decided distaste for garlic in the Victorian period, renewed interest in the bulb flourished briefly in England, but not as a food. British military doctors discovered what the Russians already knew—that it had been widely used as an antibiotic. In 1916, during ferocious fighting in World War I, the British government paid handsome prices for garlic bulbs used on the front lines in poultices applied to open or infected wounds.

The British Empire of course no longer exists. When Britons travel today they are merely impressionable tourists exposed to local culture and cookery. Rumor has it that British tourist exposure to the variety of spices in our modern world precipitated new interest in garlic in England. Yet, after a recent trip to England a friend of mine says, "They (the British) have no particular flair for spices." This was how Anne and I felt on our first visit to England a number of years back.

Our stay in London was highlighted by three events: attending a performance of Handel's Messiah at St. Martin in the Fields Church; seeing Ralph Richardson and John Gielgud together in Harold Pinter's "No Man's Land"; and dining at a Hungarian restaurant that was a breath of fresh garlic. Until we found the restaurant we dined on typical English fare, which once incredibly included rice, mashed potatoes and beans on the same plate. The only drinkable wine in the restaurants we could afford was cheap, sweet German white wine referred to by the British as "hock." At the Hungarian restaurant we ate garlic-laced blood sausage and drank blood red, deeply rich Hungarian wine on more than one occasion, and at a reasonable price.

Pockets of garlic resistance remain in parts of the world today: to some in Korea, garlic eating is a sign of poverty and ignorance, and many Anglo-influenced people still consider the smell of garlic on the breath a deficiency in social grace. Yet the plant has been generally vindicated, winning wide acceptance for its medicinal and culinary benefits from east to west and north to south. Garlic is a widely grown crop in all climates.

On this side of the Atlantic garlic was mainly disdained by Calvinists and their offspring until, in the late nineteenth and early twentieth centuries waves of immigration, particularly of Mediterranean people, brought new status to garlic in major American cities. The potent, intoxicating smells emanating from kitchens in urban homes were the smells that first-generation immigrants passed on to second generation hyphenated Americans. One of the aromas often remembered fondly by old-time Italians is the smell of soup, and few soups are as wonderful as the following.

Known in some circles as "wedding soup" variations of this soup appear often at Italian celebratory events. A glass of cool, fruity white wine is the perfect accompaniment.

INGREDIENTS TO SERVE TWO
4 cloves garlic, chopped
3 tbl. olive oil
1 onion, chopped
1 small frying chicken (or 1 Cornish hen)
1 head of escarole, cleaned and chopped
2 carrots, diced
1½ quart chicken or vegetable stock
½ cup dry Marsala
3 quarts water
2 cups of egg pastina (tiny pasta)
1 tbl. each of chopped basil and parsley
freshly grated Reggiano cheese
ground black pepper to taste

Mix ½ quart stock with ¼ cup wine into a soup pot. First remove the skin and then place the chicken or hen into the pot. Turn heat to medium, cover and cook from twenty-five to thirty minutes. Take the poultry out of the pot and place it on a chopping board to cool.

Sauté the onion in 1 tbl. olive oil until the onion is translucent, then add 2 tbl. olive oil, garlic, carrots and lay the escarole on top; sauté for five minutes to seven minutes, or until the escarole is nicely wilted.

Mix the herbs and vegetables into the soup pot, add the rest of the wine, cover and simmer.

Break up the chicken or hen meat into little pieces. Be sure to discard ALL the bones. Put the poultry pieces into the soup pot, stir and simmer for about half an hour.

Bring the water to a boil. When the water is raging, throw in the pastina and let it cook for ten minutes; then strain it. Save the water so that you can add some of it to the soup, should it be too thick for your taste.

Add a serving of pastina into each soup bowl; then pour the soup over it, sprinkle with grated cheese and black pepper to taste.

*W*E COULD, IN THE UNITED STATES, *make as great a variety of wines as are made in Europe, not exactly the same kinds, but doubtless as good.*

—THOMAS JEFFERSON [3]

*F*IFTEENTH AND SIXTEENTH CENTURY Spanish explorers brought Vitis vinifera vines to the New World. In the sixteenth and seventeenth centuries Spanish clergy introduced the mission grape to parts of South and North America.

Not to be outdone, and in an attempt to develop their own wine colonies, the British set out to plant vines in the eastern part of the New World. But the European vines could survive only under two conditions: the climate had to be warm or at least moderate and dry; and there had to be no competing indigenous grape vines. Early attempts to grow European vines in humid Virginia, the Carolinas and Florida in the seventeenth century all met with failure, even with the help of hired "vignerons" from France.

By the turn of the eighteenth century the Mediterranean had again become the center of the world's wine trade, but the British New World colonies still had no wine industry. Great amounts of Madeira were shipped from Portugal to British America, where it received preferential tax treatment over sherry and port well into the early nineteenth century. Madeira was implicated in a tax revolt nearly a decade before the famous Boston Tea Party. British customs agents who sought to collect a tax on the wine held up a shipment of Madeira in Boston harbor. A riot ensued, and the customs agents backed down. The ship's name was *Liberty* and its owner was John Hancock.

The importance of Madeira to the colonies was due, in major part, to the wine's ability to travel well and its affinity for game meats that, in the colonies, had become an important part of the diet. One such dish was a favorite aboard ship when paired with a fine Madeira.

JUGGED HARE TO SERVE FOUR [4]

INGREDIENTS
garlic bulb, cloves separated
one large rabbit
six bacon strips
one large onion, quartered
four whole cloves
a handful of hyssop, sage and parsley
¼ tsp. mace powder
salt and pepper to taste

Cut the rabbit into serving pieces and marinate it 24 hours in Rainwater Madeira.

Stick a clove into each onion quarter.

In a jug layer the rabbit, bacon and onion, and add the garlic and spices.

Place the jug into a large pot of water (leave one inch of the top of the jug exposed). Make sure the jug is sealed tightly. Bring to a boil and then cover the pot and simmer for three hours.

Serve on a bed of crisp lettuce with a glass of Madeira Sercial.

Thomas Pellechia

$\mathcal{S}$PANISH CHRISTIAN MISSIONS had created a wine culture in arid New Mexico, Texas, and in Upper Mexico, what is now California. European grapes survived and flourished almost from the start. But for more than a century the wines were produced mainly for religious purposes.

In the East, despite frequent attempts by such luminaries as Ben Franklin, George Washington and Thomas Jefferson, European grapevines did not survive. In London, Ben Franklin befriended a charming, Tuscan-born physician-turned-merchant named Philip Mazzei—a relationship that brought about Mazzei's desire to export vines and vineyard workers to Virginia. In spite of Mazzei's failure at winegrowing in Virginia, Jefferson became one of his most loyal advocates.

While Jefferson served as Ambassador to France he traveled the country and through parts of other European countries in search of wine. (On his return to America the future third President of the United States became the first President's wine mentor, selecting and buying for Washington's cellar.) Jefferson found a lot in Europe to envy and to emulate when back in America, and he relied on Mazzei for help. He also recommended Mazzei to others who wished to plant vineyards. But neither Jefferson nor Mazzei, nor any other eighteenth century viticulturist could make nature comply.

Winter and mildew were blamed for the failed winegrowing experiments in the eastern United States, but scientists later discovered that climate was only part of the problem. A devastating vine root louse, Phylloxera vastatrix, began to attack European vineyards in the middle of the nineteenth century. The scourge was brought to Europe when American vine rootstocks sent to Europe for experimental plantings carried the root louse with them. American indigenous grapevines were naturally resistant to phylloxera, but the European vines were not, and it is likely that vinifera vines imported into America from Europe one and two centuries earlier succumbed to the same disease. The phylloxera plague nearly wiped out the whole of the European wine industry. In Madeira, the blight, coupled with an earlier mildew scourge, cut crops by as much as 90%, ultimately shutting down profitable Madeira wine exports to the United States.

Garlic, Wine and Olive Oil

Scientists halted the phylloxera scourge in Europe by grafting European vines on to American phylloxera-resistant rootstocks, a practice that continues today. But while Europe appeared to be losing its wine industry, America finally developed one.

In the mid-nineteenth century the first successful wine industries in the U.S. began in the Midwest and in the Finger Lakes region of New York State. The new wine industries relied on German and French winemakers but did not rely on Vitis vinifera grapevines. Instead, the early American wine industries used native American and American field hybrid grapevines to produce still and sparkling wines. The field hybrids established themselves when, during earlier experiments with Vitis vinifera, some vinifera cross-bred with native vines on their own.

Meanwhile, the mid-nineteenth century gold rush sparked new viticultural interest on the West Coast as immigrants—Germans, Italians and Eastern Europeans—made their way to California. California climate was conducive to Vitis vinifera, but until German immigrants introduced a larger selection of European grapes, the mission grape was the primary California grape crop, and its wine quality seemed always to disappoint.

In 1920, the American wine industry came crashing down, brought to its knees by the Volstead Act (Prohibition). The few wineries that remained did so under license to produce sacramental wine. Since the legislation offered little in the way of compensation or alternative for wine producers, Prohibition caused millions of dollars in lost wine businesses suffered at both ends of the country.

By the time of Repeal in 1933, Prohibition had produced both big losers and big winners: the losers were legitimate wine and other alcohol producers, the winners were organized crime and individual states, each profiting from a monopoly on alcohol distribution; the former had its monopoly during Prohibition, the latter acquired its monopoly as a result of Repeal which gave each state the right to regulate the production, taxing, distribution and sale of alcohol.

Today, Italy, France, Germany, Spain, Portugal, Greece and Eastern European countries, all once provinces of the Roman Empire, remain important wine-producing nations; as it did with the famous vintage of 121 BC, Italy today is out-pacing many of its European neighbors with innovative, high quality wine production. It is possible that about half the world's Vitis vinifera grape varieties reside in Italy alone.

Other important wine producing countries include Chile, Argentina, Australia and South Africa. Home wine industries in Israel, Cyprus and Greece also thrive, plus Russia, and some of its bordering neighbors, still produce wine. East Asian countries produce no appreciable quantity of wine, and of course Moslem countries claim no longer to produce wine, even those countries situated next door to wine's origins.

In North America, California, New York, Washington and Oregon lead in wine production (but wine is produced in nearly all the fifty states). And Canada hosts a couple of fine wine-producing regions too.

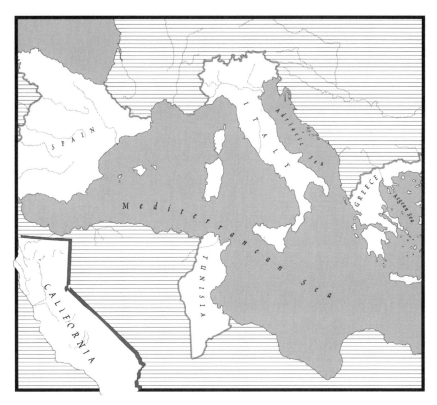

MAP OF MAJOR OLIVE PRODUCERS, INCLUDING CALIFORNIA, WHOSE OLIVES ARE CONSUMED IN THE U.S.

*D*URING THE MIDDLE AGES northern and eastern Europeans mainly cooked with animal fat, leaving the more valuable olive oil to service heating, cleansing and industrial needs. Later, great amounts of olive oil went to England during the Victorian era—it was instrumental as lubricant to the industrial revolution, and was used as a fine polish for jewelry. The olive as food seems to have been confined to the Mediterranean.

In many eastern Mediterranean communities the olive was served as an appetizer, while western Mediterraneans used it for cooking. Spain was one of the most important olive oil producers of the Roman provinces and is believed to have been using olive oil as a cooking medium for at least 2,000 years; the country remains at the top of olive oil importance today.

In the sixteenth century Spanish explorers brought the olive to Peru and to Chile. In the eighteenth century Spanish Franciscan missions brought olive trees to Mexico and into Upper Mexico (California) where they unfortunately remained a mere curiosity for a couple of centuries.

Claiming the olive was more important to the diet than bread, Thomas Jefferson planted olive trees at Monticello in the eighteenth century, but was disappointed by their failure to survive. Jefferson also sent a few hundred olive cuttings from Provence (another premium olive oil producer) to South Carolina; twenty five years later he complained that not one olive orchard existed.

Australia received the olive in the latter part of the nineteenth century and South Africa began to cultivate it in 1903. But each country has yet to produce great quantities of olives.

With the right climate and economic conditions for olive oil production, California is poised to embark on major olive cultivation, and the state has the Mediterranean both to thank for its olive trees and to compete with for the American market. Serious olive cultivation began in California in the late nineteenth century. Today, the bulk of California olive production goes to low-end, almost tasteless canned olives, and the state's low volume of olive oil production is confined to premium oils at premium prices. So when an American tastes olive oil today, it is primarily an import, and the odds are that the bulk of that oil is Spanish.

Italy claims the greatest number of olive trees in the European Economic Community, but most of the oil from those trees stays home. The majority of olive oil cans exported to the United States with the words "Product of Italy" on them are mainly blends of oils produced throughout the Mediterranean; they are packed in Italy and shipped overseas. Spain makes up the bulk of the blends, followed by Greece and the rest of the Mediterranean (Tunisia is an important supplier to Italy's packers). Spain, Greece and Tunisia are especially unhappy about the situation, since they produce good oil on their own.

For most of the decade of the 1990s, 45% of olive products

consumed in the United States were produced in Spain; the rest broke down as follows: Italy 25%, Greece 20%, the rest of the Mediterranean 9.5%, California .5%. Yet, Americans look to Italy as the benchmark for premium olive oil production. Certainly, Italians have known for a long time how best to treat olive oil, and they seem to know all too well how best to market it in America.

ROMAN RECIPE FOR FENNEL IN OLIVE OIL DIP [5]

INGREDIENTS
olive oil
salt
ground black pepper

Mix the ingredients in a bowl. Dip the wide bulb end of fennel into the olive oil and taste.

MY MOTHER'S VARIATION OF THE ABOVE:

INGREDIENTS
olive oil
wine vinegar
crushed garlic
ground black pepper

Mix the ingredients in a bowl. Dip the wide bulb end of fennel into the mix and taste.

PART IV

Journey's End

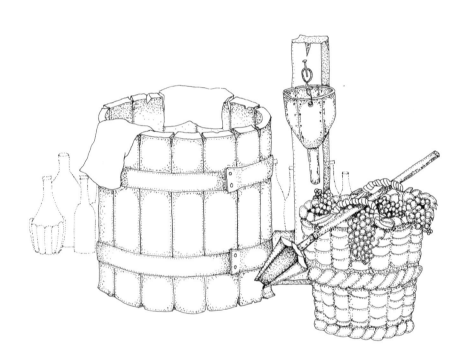

−8−

Immigration

WITH TWO HOURS TO GO before I was to catch an overnight train bound for Paris from the train station in Milan's downtown district, I went shopping for food. I explored the markets where sausages and cheeses hung, olives rested in large briny bins and freshly baked breads and pastries beckoned from their fitted berths in counters under glass. It would be my dinner stash for the train ride, and it was made complete with a last stop at the wine shop.

A beautiful Italian woman took the seat next to me in the second class section of the train. A nicely dressed man and woman were seated across from us—they were not together. The man spoke Italian but the conductor had trouble understanding his accent. The woman spoke only German. We acknowledged one another's presence with a smile, stuffed our gear in overhead and under-the-seat compartments, settled our reading material and curled into our seats, taking on the character of the solitary traveler each of us was.

About an hour into the journey I grew hungry, so from one of my bags I pulled the bread and salami I had bought in the market. The woman in the seat next to me, still holding her book in front of her, followed my moves with her eyes, all the while with a smile on her face. As I began to eat she reached under her seat to remove some cheese and bread, gesturing an offer of food to me. Then the man and woman in the seat across from us took out their stashes and, with hand gestures, offered my Italian seating partner and me some of what they had. Soon, eight hands, numerous salami and cheeses and various shapes and sizes of bread flew back and forth.

I reached for the bottle of wine in my bag, then held it up with a smile, adding four cups from a pack of cups I had with me. The man reciprocated with a bottle of wine from his bag, besting me with an offer of four efficiently packed wineglasses, which is when I discovered he was Swiss.

For the next few hours, amidst the smell of garlic and between groans of ecstasy over the food and drink, we engaged in lively conversation with hand signals and broken English, Italian, French and German until, on by one, we drifted off to sleep.

Traveling with the proper provisions is a universal need. Like entombed Egyptian princes on their journey into the unknown, thousands of nineteenth and early twentieth century Italian immigrants took with them their beloved foods to comfort them during the arduous journey across the Atlantic. I can imagine the powerful smells that blanketed the steerage passage sections of the ships bound for Ellis Island in the late nineteenth century. From inside the large pockets of ragged coats soothing aromas must have wafted across the bough—of sausages, salami and cheeses from the villages left behind. Certainly many tried to make the trip without breaking one bottle of the local village wines they had concealed in their gear. Perhaps, too, a few moistened and refreshed themselves with an olive oil bath just before boarding the cramped, brutal deck of the ship, and some rubbed on olive oil during the voyage to prevent their skin from petrifying in the salt air.

Italy had become a unified nation only in the latter part of the nineteenth century, so customs and dialects remained diverse, which made it difficult for people from one region to converse with people from another. But the sound of ecstasy is the same in any language, and those sounds must have been heard on board as Italian immigrants ate light but comforting meals.

Like the four passengers who met on that train from Milan to Paris, food was the tie that bound Italian immigrants who, after spending weeks cramped in the unwelcoming ship, had then to learn to live together in the crowded city streets of 'Merica. From the late nineteenth century to the end of World War II, American city ghettos housed Italian immigrants who spoke varying dialects, read their own newspapers, kept many of their Old World customs, ate their food and drank their wines. In many cases, whole city neighborhoods were home to insular groups from the same village or from the same region of the Italian mainland or Sicily. Often, however, Italians from many parts of Italy wound up crowded together in a few American city blocks.

Aboard those ships of immigrants were my ancestors and the many other immigrants who crowded into Brooklyn. Neapolitans held the majority, but my neighborhood also hosted people from Palermo, Calabria and Rome which meant that the culture and foods where I grew up were both similar and varied, and I can still see, smell and taste them, especially since I cook many of those dishes in my kitchen today.

My journey from the tenement to a modern-day kitchen speaks to a previous culture of food that was lost in America but is being rediscovered.

INGREDIENTS FOR A SURVIVAL PACKAGE ON A JOURNEY
garlic laced salami
a jar of extra virgin olive oil (for dipping bread)
hard cheeses
fresh olives
bread
wine
bottled mineral water
a Swiss Army knife and a cup—or four wine glasses
perhaps the luxury of a fork, a plate and some black pepper
some leak-proof plastic bags and a large carry-on bag

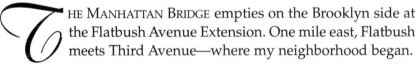

*T*HE MANHATTAN BRIDGE empties on the Brooklyn side at the Flatbush Avenue Extension. One mile east, Flatbush meets Third Avenue—where my neighborhood began.

—9—

The Neighborhood

*I*T WAS AN ITALIAN-AMERICAN SLIVER of the Park Slope section—how it came to be called South Brooklyn is a mystery, since it is on the north end of the borough. The neighborhood stretches nearly two miles south and three city blocks east. Prospect Park is at its outer eastern boundary. The famous Jewish neighborhoods of Eastern Parkway and Flatbush, where I made my Fuller Brush deliveries, border the north and east side of the park. Every one of the sixty plus blocks in my neighborhood housed hundreds of people, and most residents lived their daily lives within a three or four block radius.

The 1960s and my generation turned out to be the end of the line for the Italian neighborhood and its connection to the "old country", but from the early part of this century and into the late 1950s the neighborhood housed first and second-generation immigrants. The immigrants imparted to the "bambini" (my generation) as much of the old ways as they could, including the food, which for me was the most important of all the traditions.

At our table during special family gatherings, my mother had a favorite story she often told, between courses of homemade ravioli and steaming pots of shellfish. I don't claim to remember the actual event—I was five years old when it took place—but I heard the story often enough for it to take up residence in a corner of my mind where fantasy meets reality. The story reveals both my early bent toward self-expression, and a clue as to how long ago I began to cultivate respect for the kitchen.

My aunt Fannie filtered no thought between the time it entered her mind and when it left her tongue. My mother, who was no slouch in the self-expression department, seemed always to come up short around her older sister. Perhaps this was so because when her mother died a relatively young woman, my grandfather took my mother out of the Bronx school she attended, which she loved, and designated her housekeeper for the family. As the younger of the two girls in the family she became cook and cleaning lady, suffering all the injustices that comes with that position. Anyway, aunt Fannie's terrorizing tactics, and her need to have the last word, created great apprehension in my mother whenever she planned a journey from Brooklyn to visit her sister in the Bronx.

It was indeed a journey from Brooklyn to the Bronx. The BMT subway line, a local, which we got a block away from our tenement, did not go to the Bronx. To get to that rarified destination one had to change at 34th Street in Manhattan for the IND line, and since, like ours, aunt Fannie's tenement was near a local stop, the trip could only be accomplished by taking local trains the whole way, for nearly two hours.

The whole of the Bronx was alerted of my mother's arrival as soon as she and her sister began to converse—a genetic misfortune made the two hard of hearing. Each spoke louder than the other, and since they each were incessant talkers, their conversations were a booming barrage.

On one hot 1950 summer Saturday my mother took me on the long journey to aunt Fannie's. During most of our visits, Fannie's daughter Rose stayed out of the line of fire by washing windows or some such thing until dinner time, making an appearance every so often to refill glasses with iced tea and to rebut something her mother had said. Uncle Louie spent his afternoons at the "beer garden," as aunt Fannie called it, arriving home at precisely five minutes before dinner, after which he either fell off to sleep or found a reason to get out of the apartment again.

On this particular trip my mother and I endured the usual afternoon harangue relatively unscathed, but then we had to succumb to an aunt Fannie meal. Fannie never learned how to cook. The first course of her dinner on this summer day was a dish of limp pasta, which she followed with leather-bound meat accompanied by what my aunt claimed was spinach. Uncle Louie took more wine than food, growing less and less verbal as the wine bottles emptied. My mother and cousin Rose ate, politely, with alternating dabs at their food and head nods to aunt Fannie who could talk, chew and swallow at the same time. I pushed my food around the plate, ate a little and then pushed some more; my mother said I had the look of a boy longing for a dog under the table to feed. It was an uneventful dinner—until I took a bite of the green stuff.

The way my mother told it, with a mixture of pride and incredulity in her voice, I took a forkful of spinach in my mouth then quickly spit it back onto the plate. Before aunt Fannie could react I blurted that the spinach was gritty and had not been properly washed. Surprised and oddly at a loss for words, my aunt stuttered, blamed her daughter for the impropriety and commanded me to eat the spinach anyway. I told her that none of the vile vegetable would go into my mouth until it was properly prepared, which I explained would be impossible for that particular batch of spinach since it had already been cooked beyond recognition to a gritty, bitter glob of granular mush.

My mother was proud of me that day, she said, because I expressed the plain truth with that particular family-inherited brand of indiscretion. Happy as she was over the incident, my mother always ended the story wondering about the source of my culinary insight, since none of the other male members of our family—and there are many—showed any inclination or talent for matters of *la cucina*.

SPINACH IN GARLIC AND OIL

INGREDIENTS
3 cloves garlic, minced
1 Spanish onion, chopped
½ pound of fresh spinach, cleaned thoroughly
2 tbl. olive oil
½ cup white wine, plus some more on hand
1 tbl. sugar
1 lemon
ground black pepper to taste

Sauté the onion in olive oil until the onion is translucent.

Separate the spinach into individual leaves and put aside.
Mix the sugar and wine and add it to the onion. Let the liquid in the pan reduce to half over medium heat, and then add the spinach and garlic, wilt the spinach (3 minutes) do not let it become mush. Add a little more wine if it becomes dry in the pan.

Serve with lemon wedges and sprinkle with ground pepper to taste.

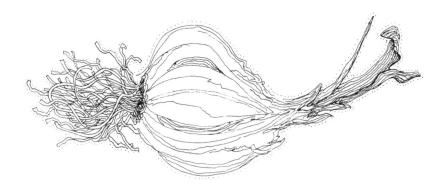

HE POPULATION OF ROME was absorbed by its bread and circuses.

—JUVENAL, 2ND CENTURY [1]

*T*HE ANCIENTS shopped for food and clothing at outdoor fairs and markets. The markets of Mesopotamia, Babylon, Persia and China overflowed with traders, local merchants, shoppers and volumes of that which local farmers and tradesmen could not produce, brought to them by barges that scurried down the Euphrates and Tigris or caravans that traversed the famous Silk Road. The Romans took the custom further when they built the Forum, a multi-level open-air structure that hosted museums, libraries, municipal courts, stock markets, banks, department stores, specialty craft shops, restaurants, food markets and even a pond where fish were raised and sold for food. The food markets displayed produce from the Italic peninsula as well as foods imported from Rome's trading partners and provinces. The food market was the noisiest, most bustling part of the Forum for this is where plebeian and aristocrat converged to trade and to procure sustenance. Haggling and argument often preceded the deal.

To someone just "off the boat" my neighborhood in the 1950s could well have been the village left behind. Italian, or at least dialects of it, were spoken loudly on the streets, on the horse-drawn wagons of Nick the ice man, Tony the junk man, the men who sharpened knives and those who delivered coal or seltzer. Fifth Avenue was our Forum.

The women—always women—walked only a couple of blocks along Fifth, to the primary shopping area between Union and Carroll Streets. In those two city blocks were the butcher, seafood store, baker, produce stand, wine shop, donut shop, pizza restaurant and one of the many neighborhood taverns. The pasta store was there too with freshly-made pasta right next to the pork store and its freshly stuffed sausages which was close to the dairy shop with its freshly-made mozzarella. The market also included a neighborhood funeral parlor, to pay respects to those no longer able to smell and taste the wonders around us. The undertaker was the younger brother of a wealthy doctor—a fine arrangement. The poolroom was also on the block, but that is another story. Not far from the poolroom you could buy men's clothing or women's lingerie, a hat at the milliner's and household goods at the hardware store. At the corner we shopped at the pharmacy for coke syrup and other old-time remedies, and at the cigar-candy-newspaper store, the old men bought small, dark, twisted Italian stogies to puff on while they grew angry at the *Daily Mirror*, *Daily News* or *Il Progresso*. The bank was there too, where some managed every so often to save a few cents out of their hard-earned paychecks. Not far away was the dry cleaner, for maintaining the one good suit and dress for Saturday night out.

The market hummed daily with the southern Italian dialect of shoppers and shopkeepers: "oquant ecost?" (how much) was the question, "eh, tus amadiul" (you are a crook) was the response no matter what the answer.

The dialect spoken in my neighborhood placed great importance on vowels, so much so that they were often taken from the ending of words and put at the beginning. And many consonants were also re-made: the "p" sound changed to a "b", and the rolling "r" in Italian was transformed into the sound of "ad"; to my mother and her contemporaries pizza became abitz, ricotta was adecort, oregano sounded like odaygan, calamari was called icalamar, and spicchi d'aglio (cloves of garlic) was pronounced ispeak odal.

Friday pay envelopes ensured an overflowing Saturday market, where the proper placement of vowels and consonants were lost to the incredible volume. This is when the ever-present hand and facial gestures became important.

Saturday crowds were close. Waiting was a time-consuming art, especially at Franco's butcher shop where there were maybe two chairs to accommodate the dozen or so people in line with their numbers held tightly in the palms of their hands on a stub they checked after each ring of the cash register to see who would be next.

Franco was a true customer servant. Caught between the need to make a profit and the need to satisfy customers, he had to be resourceful and cunning. The women exercised power over him—

they commanded the thickness of the cut and dictated how much fat to trim. But Franco bought and sold meat by the pound, including fat and bones and he was not about to let any of it go to waste. He was sure to tell the ladies about a recipe that made use of excess fat or how to cook the bone for stock.

One of the most active pieces of equipment at Franco's was the meat grinder. Pork, veal and beef were ground to make the best meatballs and the best Italian meatloaf. It was at the meat grinder that the butcher's temper was likely to flare. After a long and hot debate over whether he had cut enough fat off the chunks of meat to be ground, Franco was then subjected to close scrutiny as he ground the meat. Whether he suggested two grinds or three, la signora, making a hand or face gesture, wanted one more; if he suggested more pork than veal, she grimaced for more veal. And as he bickered and cut, the butcher kept an eye on the growing line of customers waiting, certain he would not get home until late that night. I focused on the grinder, fascinated by how chunks of meat went in one end and small, stringy pieces of meat came out the other.

I often sat on the ledge in the window, whiling the wait time making patterns in the sawdust on the floor while trying to fend off the hair rubs and cheek pulls of my mother's shopping cronies as they cooed in dialect "che bel obambin" (a handsome baby). Perhaps in a show of male solidarity, or perhaps because my mother paid him for it, one of Franco's helpers often gave me a hot dog to nibble on while I waited.

After a few bouts with the women, Franco showed his frustration. I could often hear him mumbling to himself Italian words that I was not supposed to use.

Buonocore's produce stand around the corner from Franco's was part indoor and part outdoor market. The large, dark, smiling proprietor was always happy to give me fresh, snappy green beans or carrots to munch on while I waited for my mother to do her shopping. He treated me nicely because I was classmate and spelling bee equal of his daughter.

Buonocore's overflowed with wooden crates of garlic, onion, shallot, fennel, broccoli, many kinds of peppers, cauliflower, cabbages, tomatoes, arugula, escarole, basil, parsley, carrot and all kinds of dried and fresh beans, plus fruits like lemons, oranges, apples, peaches, plums, pears and figs. The store had more stock in winter than in summer—in summer Nick competed with family gardens. How he brought in the many greens and fruits in winter and how he got away with the exorbitant winter prices was often the topic of conversation at Buonocore's—the ladies complaining, the proprietor boasting. Of course, in our neighborhood garlic was in greater demand than supply. No matter the season, Nick always had bushels of large garlic bulbs.

To shop was to pick, pluck, pinch, tuck, fondle, role, squeeze (when allowed) and—most important of all—bicker about the price. To appease the women, fourteen often equaled a dozen, or a pound was topped up with another eighth of a pound, especially at the end of a long Saturday when, tired from the ordeal they had undergone, the shopkeepers were also aware they would be closed the following day and that they had to move whatever would spoil. We were by no means wealthy, yet my mother seemed always to shop in the early morning, foregoing the potential bargains of later in the day. She claimed that in the morning odds were better that she would find everything she set out to buy, some of which could be gone by late day. I knew better. She went to market early in the morning to get in a full day of talking to friends—to shop was also to socialize.

The closest I have come in my adult life to the Saturday market of the old neighborhood was in southern Tehran, in that mysterious, swarming place known as the bazaar. In the bazaar you can buy items from the luxurious—intricate tribal carpets made by hand in the many small villages of the country—to the mundane—handmade lamps carved and adorned to give them as hideous and gaudy a look of any velvet Elvis painting in America. At the bazaar Iranians picked, plucked, pinched, tucked, rolled, squeezed and—most of all—bargained, the universal habits that are as old as civilization.

But the modern bazaar no longer represents everyday shopping in the everyday world of local communities, especially in the major cities. When we shopped in our northern Tehran neighborhood, we shopped for dinner staples in markets similar to the ones my mother and I shopped. On the streets and in those shops I often felt like the little boy in Brooklyn, listening but unable to under-

Garlic, Wine and Olive Oil

stand the spoken language, yet able to fully comprehend the language of shopping, the language that includes picking, plucking and hand and facial gestures of approval or disapproval. Of course, no butcher's helper or produce man ever gave us anything to eat while we waited for our turn in line. And for the two years we lived in Tehran we could not buy pork, which is not eaten in Moslem countries, nor could we buy veal, which was too expensive. For meatballs, we made do with ground beef and lamb. But this is how my mother made meatballs:

INGREDIENTS FOR MEATBALLS TO FEED AT LEAST FOUR
8 cloves minced garlic
3 tbl. olive oil, plus 2
1 pound lean ground pork, veal and beef combined
1 egg
½ cup plain bread crumbs, plus ¼ cup
½ cup chopped parsley, plus ¼ cup
ground black pepper

Flatten the meat out on a board. Place the garlic in the center of the meat. Crack-open an egg and blend it into the meat and garlic for a few minutes. Add ¼ cup bread-crumbs and roll the mixture into a ball.

Make a crevice in the center of the ball and add another ¼ cup of breadcrumbs and ¼ cup parsley. Knead for a few minutes. You want the consistency to be loose but not wet. You should have that about now; if not, add some more breadcrumbs, slowly, then add the rest of the parsley and the pepper and mix well.

Roll the mixture into a large ball and then break off chunks of meat and roll into small meatballs, from 1 to 1½-inch diameter. When all the meatballs are rolled, cook them in olive oil in a cast iron pan, on medium heat, rolling them around until each side is nicely browned. You might find you need more olive oil to accommodate all the meatballs; just add more oil to the pan as you continue to cook the rest of the meatballs.

Lay out cooked meatballs on a paper towel to drain.

Before adding the meatballs to a pasta sauce, eat one. See if you do not agree that a dry meatball prepared this way makes a marvelous appetizer.

*I*N THE NINETEENTH CENTURY, when the largest number of Italians came to America, they left farms behind to work in the growing industrial culture of America. But farming was part of the peasant genetic make-up so some immigrants went west or to fertile regions of the Northeast, where they established vineyards, fruit orchards and farms. Those who landed in urban communities nurtured their farming genes in the backyard.

Our next door neighbor, Ralph, was a road crewman by day, and a gardener in spirit and in the evening. The medium-built, darkly handsome, volatile man had three daughters but no sons. I worked with Ralph in the garden as part of our symbiotic relationship. With plants, and with me, he was a patient nurturer who knew that growing things had their own method and their own pace. It was our job to feed, to weed and to wait for the plants to mature.

"Give it a good soaking" he used to say when I watered. I was tentative, not wanting to drown the plants. Ralph commanded me to feed the plants "an inch of water a week." He insisted that we water towards the end of the day, so the plant leaves would not suffer a shock when cool water met the hot rays of the sun on their surface. This was his explanation for waiting until after supper to water, but I know he also wanted to be there, to both be a part of the watering and weeding and to teach me the lessons that gardening had to offer.

He taught me the joy one could get from growing plants that begin as the tiniest of seeds, to end in their fullest, majestic purpose as food. From Ralph I learned that you can perform work for money and you can perform work to build character and spirit, and that the latter is preferable. He taught me about accepting the slowness and sureness of gardening in a good year and the disappointment of gardening in a bad year. He taught me how to tell when a garlic stalk signals it is time to dig up the bulbs. I learned these things from Ralph by the process of osmosis, by listening and watching in the tiny backyard garden that stole a narrow stretch of Brooklyn sunlight.

We grew tomatoes, arugula, escarole, peppers, corn, watermelons, cantaloupe, squash, cucumbers, green beans, and other beans, parsley, basil, onions, zucchini and lots of garlic.

For my pay, I got a share of the harvest, which we usually saved for crisp, early Saturday mornings, after Ralph served breakfast of marvelously light pancakes that he loaded with real vanilla. But there were times when we ate from the garden well before harvest approached, like when zucchini flowers bloomed.

INGREDIENTS TO SERVE TWO
4 cloves garlic, pressed
5 tbl. olive oil
zucchini flowers (about six flowers for two people)
1 egg
2 tbl. milk
1 tbl. each chopped basil and oregano
pinch crushed hot red pepper
½ cup breadcrumbs
1 lemon
½ cup chopped parsley

Pick zucchini flowers before fruits set. The dish needs to be prepared from fresh flowers, so pick an hour or so before dinner.

Pour the breadcrumbs onto a flat surface. In a bowl combine the milk with the egg and mix well with a fork; then soak the flowers, one-by-one, in the mixture, lift and let the liquid drain off; then roll the flower in the breadcrumbs covering it completely. Chill for an hour.

Sauté the garlic in 2 tbl. olive oil with half the basil and oregano, plus the crushed pepper, for one minute.

Add the rest of the oil and then the breaded flowers. Cook until golden brown on all sides. When done, remove with a spatula and place the flowers in a strainer over a paper towel to drain any excess oil.

Serve with a squirt of lemon and garnish with the rest of the basil and oregano plus the parsley.

$\mathcal{U}$NLIKE RALPH, who was a second-generation Italian-American, old man Anton had come off the boat; he lived in a small house next door to us. Anton spoke extremely broken English but he got by rather well in a neighborhood where English was a second-generation language.

Vegetables were not the draw that brought me to Anton's backyard, nor was it because that is where I got my first taste of a beautiful, ripe fig from the tree that the old man wrapped in burlap for protection from Brooklyn winters. The burlap Anton used as fig wrapping started out as bags to hold the many pounds of lemons that were delivered to him throughout the summer. I knew when the lemons arrived that Nick the iceman would soon follow, and that bags of cane sugar would not be far behind. Anton was gearing up to make another batch of lemon ice for his summer-only outdoor candy and food store, and I might be summoned to help out.

First we broke up big blocks of ice with an ice pick to make smaller chunks that would fit into a chute the old man had built. Anton used an electric grinding machine to crush the ice. It had a rhythmic drone: a click and then a long period of suction-like sounds as the gears cycled, and its metronomic pace mesmerized you to a doze if you weren't careful. I poured the ice chunks into the chute and then the old man started the grinder, which churned and pushed finely crushed ice into an old wooden wine barrel that had been cut to fit under the chute.

Anton lifted the heavy bags of sugar and he squeezed the lemons, one at a time, with his juicer. We mixed the lemon, sugar and finely crushed ice and then poured and spooned the ingredients into a few cylindrical tubs made of metal. We carried the tubs of freshly made lemon ice to the front of the house, where the store was, and placed them snugly into a freezer that Anton lined with dry ice.

The resulting lemon ice was both simple and divine. No so-called Italian lemon ice I have tasted over the years has come remotely close to Anton's with its fine granular texture, perfectly balanced acid-sweetness, and crisp citrus taste, so fresh that my friends and I created the "how far can you spit the lemon pits" game. My glorious pay was one free lemon ice each day for a week

Garlic, Wine and Olive Oil

after each crush, not to mention the figs I picked off of his tree when the old man was not looking—or was he?

Anton's outdoor candy and food stand offered the neighborhood a blend of Italian and American cultures that started with his spectacular lemon ice and ended with a Manhattan Special, an Italian carbonated espresso drink. He sold snacks of fresh pine and pistachio nuts, dried ceci nuts (chickpeas), corn on the cob brushed with garlic-laced olive oil, marvelous lupini beans, (a lima-bean look alike cooked and preserved in a garlicky-salty brine) plus potatoes deep fried in olive oil.

INGREDIENTS FOR DEEP FRIED POTATOES TO SERVE TWO
4 cloves garlic, pressed
1½ quarts olive oil
two large red potatoes, cut into tall strips, with skins
salt to taste
chopped parsley as garnish

Heat the oil to 375 degrees.

Add the potatoes and garlic in a strainer and then dip the strainer into the hot oil.

When the potatoes turn golden (fifteen minutes, or so) turn off the flame, lift out the potatoes and put the oil aside to cool.

Sprinkle salt and flip the potatoes in the strainer at the same time until you cover all of them with as much salt as you desire, and until the oil stops dripping.

Serve in a plate to accompany the main dish.

Later, pour the cooled olive oil through a fine filter into a jar and refrigerate (a coffee filter will do). You can re-use it for frying as much as ten times, provided you filter and refrigerate it after each use. This is the only time you should refrigerate olive oil.

$\mathcal{A}$NTON CLOSED HIS STORE at the end of September, but he did not rest. First he had to clean the place up and winterize it; then he had to tend to his wine. I suppose Italian immigrants would have made wine at home whether or not our federal government had laws forbidding the practice, but our constitutional right to make 200 gallons a year per head of household was gladly accepted by immigrants.

The grandfathers who made wine in my neighborhood got together each year to place their order for the grapes that rolled in by truck in October. The trucks stopped at a central point on the block, then the old men climbed into the bed picking, squeezing, tasting, bickering and unloading their purchases.

Grapes were packed in heavy wooden boxes that over time became too heavy for the old men to handle. Some of us kids were always on hand to do the lifting for them. The immediate task of carrying heavy grape boxes into the cellar was unrewarding—the grapes were hardly edible—but we knew that our reward, and the reward of the whole neighborhood, awaited us in the coming Thanksgiving and Christmas holidays, when last year's wines made their appearance.

My four grandparents had all died by the time I reached the age of reason. But living so close to Anton, and being one of his favorite lemon ice workers, benefited my family and me. At holiday time the old man dropped off a gallon or two of wine. Just as natural ingredients and a perfect balance between sugar and acidity was key to the greatness of his lemon ice, so it was with many of Anton's wine. I first tasted the rich, dark, heavy wine when I was perhaps nine years old; it was cut with water but I could still feel and taste the passion the old man had put into making it. But I had already been familiarized with Anton's wine well before my first taste of it.

While they fermented their new wines the old men would bottle the wine they made the previous autumn. For the brief time between bottling the old and pumping the new into barrels, their cellars housed barrels empty of wine but filled with gloriously vinous fumes. That was when some of us kids sneaked into the cellar. We placed a stool in front of a large barrel and pulled out its

Garlic, Wine and Olive Oil

bung. Then we took turns sticking our noses into each barrel, moving along to the three, four or five barrels until, our heads floating, we could no longer take it.

If there were problems with the wine made by neighborhood grandfathers, and there sometimes were, it was for two reasons. The grapes were mostly of the lowest quality, and since they had traveled from California by rail and by truck, they were also quite old by the time they reached Brooklyn. In addition, the immigrant winemakers were men suffering the humiliations of old age; they could no longer think and act as sharply as they once did, resulting in winemaking techniques that were not always safe and sanitary. Many old timers cut homemade wines with water not just as a precaution but because many wines were volatile—you could literally see the air around an open jug, especially the ones that had gone to "aceto" half the ingredient of a simple olive oil and vinegar salad dressing.

But many wines had their moments, and I can remember the great to-do when Anton's momentous wines appeared at table. Most of the wine was red, so when it was good it fared quite well with the thick, rich tomato sauces we had during holiday dinners. It even went well with some of the traditional seafood concoctions that were an Italian Christmas Eve tradition.

HARDY FISH CHOWDER FOR FOUR

INGREDIENTS
1 garlic bulb, its cloves chopped
2 tbl. olive oil
1 large onion, chopped
4 red potatoes, cut into quarters
4 carrots, diced
1 sweet red pepper, sliced
½ pound cod filet
1 dozen medium-sized shrimp
1 pound of mussels
1 dozen little neck clams
1 dozen oysters, shucked

1 quart crushed whole tomatoes
½ cup dry Marsala
2 cups vegetable stock or water, plus more
2 tbl. each chopped basil, thyme and parsley
a few bay leaves
2 tbl. gumbo filé
crushed hot red pepper

Sauté the onion in olive oil until it is translucent; then add the garlic and sauté for 30 seconds.

Empty the crushed tomatoes into a soup or stew pot and add ¼-cup Marsala plus 1 cup vegetable stock or water.

Add the garlic, onions, other vegetables and cod fish to the stew pot, cover and simmer for ten minutes.

Add basil, thyme, parsley, bay leaf, gumbo filé and hot pepper to taste, stir and simmer for another three minutes. Add the rest of the Marsala and the rest of the stock or water, stir, cover and simmer for twenty minutes—be sure not to let the stew boil—and check for moisture. Perhaps you will want to add more stock or water. Make the decision based on whether you want soup or chowder, that is, a liquid dish or a thick dish.

Clean the mussels and clams by running them under cold water—you must also pull the hairy-like "beard" from the mussel shells. Make sure the mussels and clams are alive. An open mussel doesn't necessarily mean a dead mussel. Hold the shell under running water for a few seconds then place it in the sink. If it is alive, the mussel will close its shell. If the shell does not budge, toss that mussel. The clam shells should be shut tight. Do not eat a clam if the shell is open before you cook it.

Get the shrimp out of their shells, de-veined if you like, and rinse them under cold water.

Check the potatoes in the stew pot. When you can stick a fork through them with complete ease, throw the clams in the pot.

Steam the mussels separately. When they open, put the mussels aside and check to see if the clam shells have opened; when they have, throw the shrimp and oysters into the pot. Cook for 1 minute, add the mussels, stir vigorously wait thirty seconds and then ladle

Garlic, Wine and Olive Oil

into big bowls accompanied by small bowls for the spent shells. Serve with a chunk of baguette or thick country bread, and since you will not have Anton's wine, try another bold red.

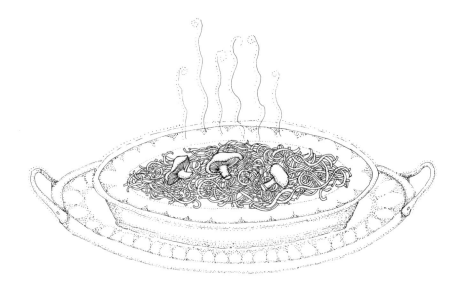

*I*N THE 1950s AND 1960s Prince Pasta Company trucks traversed the streets of New York with a large sign on them claiming something to the effect that Wednesday is macaroni day. In our neighborhood Prince was short a few days—Wednesday and Sunday, and sometimes Friday, were macaroni days, and we ate a lot of spaghetti.

My favorite spaghetti dish was one we ate only on Friday, the night meat was forbidden to pre-Vatican II Catholics, and only in summer, the time of year Maryland blue crabs are in season. It was messy, breaking crab shells which had been immersed in tomato sauce, but it was an incredibly scrumptious feast of flavors, combining the acidity of the sauce with hot red pepper and the sweetness of crab meat.

My mother put on a large pot of tomato sauce, with additional hot pepper, and then boiled water for the crabs. She took the live crabs out of the wooden box—carefully—and threw them in boiling water. When the shells turned red, the crabs were ready. She then immersed the crabs in the sauce, stirring them in to get a good coating. She boiled water for the pasta, and when the spaghetti was done she topped up our plates of pasta with a generous helping of sauce and crabs. Then we passed a couple of nutcrackers around the table to crack the crab shells—to my mother's consternation, I sometimes used my teeth for this purpose.

On Sundays we ate many different kinds of pasta: cavatelli (cylindrical, ribbed pasta, which reminded me of the Lone Ranger bullets that came with my six-shooter); ravioli (ricotta-filled), lasagna (layered with sausage and ricotta); ziti (tubed, sometimes ribbed); penne regate (tubed, ribbed and cut at an angle).

Tomato sauce for Sunday dinner usually was already on the stove by the time I got home from nine o'clock Mass. After breakfast we spent the rest of the morning in anticipation of the mid-afternoon Sunday supper. Many from the old country believed tomato sauce had to simmer for hours for spices and flavors to meld, which is true if you are making a southern Italian ragu, which we often ate on Sundays.

On special Sundays or holidays we made prized ravioli from scratch, an all morning family affair that sharpened everyone's

Garlic, Wine and Olive Oil

appetite. My mother and one of my three sisters prepared the dough with the prescribed blend of water and egg to flour, slapping it on a large wooden board where it was rolled, over and over, with a wooden rolling pin. It took plenty of time to get it right, plus about two hours of refrigeration.

We bought freshly made ricotta cheese at the "latticini freschi" shop on Fifth Avenue. My mother and a sister blended egg, parsley and pepper to the cheese while one other sister and I used an old jelly jar to make circle cut-outs in the rolled and flattened, cool dough. Then we spooned a portion of the ricotta mix on one half of the circle, folded the other half of the circle over it and crimped the edges of the pasta with our fingers to close the individual ravioli shut.

Another special holiday dish, lasagna, was also a big event. The difficult task with lasagna was to create four alternating layers of ricotta, sausage, and sauce, between the wide, flat dough while keeping the dish filling but light; a task that was often met with great success, especially when my oldest sister, Rose, prepared it.

If I wasn't helping out with the ravioli, my hunger pangs and I went outside to play with the other children. Between breakfast and mid-afternoon the aroma of garlic and tomato sauce wafting from hundreds of tenements on the block hung like a pleasant mist. None of the children were up to full steam, our games made less energetic, our pace more languid, our minds concentrated on getting back for supper.

These days I make a quick tomato sauce.

INGREDIENTS FOR PASTA IN TOMATO SAUCE TO SERVE TWO
THE SAUCE
3 cloves garlic, minced
1 tbl. olive oil
32 oz. chopped tomatoes from the garden (sans skins) or unsalted canned tomatoes
2 oz. tomato paste (optional, if you want thickness)
2 tbl. honey (to balance the acidity of the tomato)
½ cup of aged red wine (the wine you will serve with the meal)
2 tbl. each chopped basil, oregano, thyme

a couple of fresh bay leaves
a dried hot red pepper and all its seeds
parsley for garnish

To skin fresh tomatoes boil up a pot of water and then dunk the tomatoes in a strainer into the water for thirty to forty seconds. The skins should be easy to slip off the tomato. You also need to cut out and toss the eyes of the tomato. Some like to seed also, but that takes a lot of time.

Sauté garlic on low heat in olive oil for one minute. Deglaze the pan with a little wine. Add the garlic and whatever oil remains in the pan, the tomato, half the basil, oregano and thyme, bay leaves, hot pepper and the rest of the wine to a saucepot. Stir well and put on a low to medium flame for about half an hour. The sauce is ready. Serve it over pasta and sprinkle with the remaining basil, oregano and thyme, plus the parsley for garnish.

THE PASTA
16 oz. pasta (any of your favorite)
2½ quarts water
1 tsp. olive oil
half a lemon

Add the olive oil to the water (to keep pasta from sticking together while cooking) and add squeezed half of a lemon to the water (in place of salt); then boil the water. When the water is raging add the pasta. Cook for eight to ten minutes. Check for consistency—it should be firm and chewy. Strain the pasta (it will cook more while straining) and serve in bowls topped up with grated cheese (if you like) and garnished sauce, in that order.

Garlic, Wine and Olive Oil

*T*HE MAJORITY of early Italian immigrants in the United States were from the Mezzogiorno, the name given to the southern region of the peninsula. This is where poverty was concentrated in the country so these are the people who sought to flee to a better life. Italian-American cooking, therefore, was influenced mostly by southern Italians. Meals laden with thick, red tomato sauce became known as Italian food in the United States and they became the staples in many Italian restaurants across the country. Often, meals with a northern Italian pedigree were treated the southern way— breaded veal cutlets smothered in tomato sauce with melted cheese is a far cry from the delicately breaded veal cutlet "al la Milanese" served with a lemon wedge and parsley. I still remember the absolute joy of my first taste in 1975 of northern Italian veal dish in a Manhattan restaurant. But those kinds of restaurants were rare in those days, and back then I still had no idea that pasta could be smothered in anything but tomato sauce and still taste good.

I grew up with one type of ravioli—stuffed with ricotta cheese, and smothered in thick, rich tomato sauce. I loved it then and still love it today. The dish is one of the many in Brooklyn that married two cultures—ravioli is a northern Italian pasta. I have since learned that northern Italians prefer delicate dishes many of which, like veal, are not covered with tomato sauce. And when northern Italians do prepare sauce, even tomato sauce, it is usually delicate and simple.

In 1989, in a restaurant in Buffalo, New York, I was drawn to this menu item: Shrimp-stuffed Ravioli with Sweet Red and Yellow Pepper Sauce. I was embarrassed that I was nearly 45 years old and had never tasted ravioli stuffed with something other than cheese and smothered in something other than tomato sauce. Since then I have made the dish at home using ravioli stuffed with lobster, crab, pumpkin and sweet potato, but, oddly, never with shrimp. The dish is nice with a northern Italian crisp white wine, but it is really good with an Alsatian or Alsatian-style white wine like Gewürztraminer.

Thomas Pellechia

INGREDIENTS TO SERVE TWO
6 cloves garlic, minced
2 tbl. olive oil plus a dribble for the pasta water
half a lemon for the pasta water
ravioli of choice (8 to 10 per person)
about ⅓ cup water for every ravioli
four large sweet red peppers and four large sweet yellow
peppers, roasted*
2 tsp. each chopped basil, oregano and thyme
¼ cup white vinegar, plus more
2 tsp. granulated white sugar, plus more
½ cup freshly grated Romano cheese
¼ cup chopped parsley

*To roast the peppers cut them in half, remove the stems, seeds and fleshy insides. Lay the peppers, skin side up, on a pan and place in the oven to bake at 350 degrees for about half an hour, or until the skin blisters (try a small toaster oven). Remove and let the peppers cool, then peel the skins.

Keep the yellow peppers separate from the red ones—you will be making two sauces. Purée the peppers in a processor; again, keep the red and yellow separate.

Add 1 tbl. olive oil each to two separate sautéing pans. Put half the garlic in one pan and half in the other pan—sauté both for one minute.

Mix vinegar with sugar and taste for balance. Adjust accordingly. Add half the mixture to the puréed red peppers, the other half to the yellow peppers.

Put each pepper purée into the already garlic-sautéed pans. Add a teaspoon each of basil, oregano and thyme to each pan. Simmer on low flame while you prepare the pasta, stirring frequently.

Add a couple of drops of olive oil and the squeezed lemon to the water and boil. Cook the ravioli in boiling water. Note: if you are using frozen ravioli they are usually done when the water comes to another boil and the ravioli rise to the top of the pot; if you are using fresh ravioli, give them eight to ten minutes to cook. But always check any pasta to be sure it is the consistency you want.

Garlic, Wine and Olive Oil

As the ravioli waits on the plates take the grated cheese and mix half into the simmering pepper sauces in each pan. Turn off the heat and stir the cheese in nicely to thicken the sauce, then pour the sauce over the ravioli and garnish with parsley.

*O*UR NEIGHBORHOOD had become one of the earliest of the downtown Brooklyn Italian strongholds to succumb to change. Like surrounding Italian neighborhoods ours was mostly working class and poor with a few Italian doctors, lawyers and "wise guys" with their Simonized black cars that were bigger than most of the cold water flats in which many immigrants still resided.

At the end of the Second World War returning soldiers, helped by the G.I. Bill, set out finally to achieve the American dream—an education, a good job and their own family home. After having spent a couple of generations crowded into five-story tenements with two families per floor, in no more than four rooms for each family, people in the neighborhood began to move to better city neighborhoods or "up" to the suburbs—both Staten and Long Islands drew a lot of them. The wave of immigrants at New York harbor had subsided too, and as Italian families left the neighborhood in came new immigrants from Puerto Rico and Cuba; perhaps Puerto Ricans were not technically immigrants, but they certainly came to New York with their own culture.

By the time I entered first grade, although we still represented the majority, the Italian kids on my block had Puerto Rican friends. We all were richer for the experience—for the sugar cane that Latinos taught us Italian kids to chew in summer and for the lemon ice we taught the Puerto Rican kids to enjoy as a cool refreshment. As the face of the neighborhood changed, smells of pepperoni mingled with chorizo, the butcher sold less veal and more chicken and the produce man added plantain to his stock. But the two foods that held sway in both Latin-influenced cultures were as prevalent as ever.

The base for nearly every dinner in the myriad apartments on my block was garlic and olive oil. To walk down the block at five in the evening, as dinner cooked, was to be bombarded with the warring aromas of Italian and Spanish-style garlic dishes. The walls of those old tenements were held together by generations of solidified olive oil residue, and I can still smell the Alliacious breaths of the hundreds of olive-skinned children who blanketed the streets.

But one can live neither on garlic nor olive oil alone, nor on pasta.

The Spanish acquired the rice habit when the Arab Moors controlled most of southern Spain from the eighth century to the end of the fifteenth century. Knowing little about the rich northern Italian heritage of rice brought to the Italic peninsula by tenth-century Saracen invasions, we used to tease our Puerto Rican friends. We assumed the world ate nothing but pasta. And we thought nothing of eating pasta with beans, but rice with beans—plain crazy, until you taste it, which I did at my friend Juvenal's apartment.

INGREDIENTS FOR RICE, BEANS AND PORK TO SERVE TWO
3 cloves garlic, chopped
1 large Spanish onion, chopped
2 tbl. olive oil
½ cup of Basmati rice
8 oz. black beans
2 – 1½-inch thick center cut pork chops
flour for dusting the chops
½ cup dry Marsala
1 cup chicken stock
¼ cup chopped cilantro leaves
3 tbl. chili powder
1 roasted sweet red pepper
ground black pepper

Open part of the top of a can of black beans and place over the sink drain to rid the can of its salty liquid. Or, if you are using fresh black beans from the garden, wash them, add a pinch of baking soda and cook them in water for half an hour (do not boil); then rinse three times and put the beans aside. If you are using dried beans, follow instructions on the package for cooking.

Dust the chops on each side with flour and sprinkle them with black pepper. Cook in a skillet of 1 tbl olive oil, on each side until browned (maybe two minutes). Remove the pork chops and rest on a plate.

Bring the rice to a boil in two cups of water, then simmer until just before the rice soaks up all the water (maybe ten minutes).

Turn off the heat, cover and let sit.

Sauté onion in 1 tbl. olive oil in a large pan until it is translucent; then add the garlic and sauté 30 seconds.

Add half the chicken stock, the wine, cilantro, 1 tbl. chili powder and pork chops to the garlic and onion (rub some of the chili on the pork chops); cover and simmer on low heat for five minutes.

Turn the pork chops over add 1 tbl. chili (rub chili on the pork chop) and stir in the beans, cover and simmer on low heat, checking until the pork chops are cooked yet tender (about seven minutes).

Add the rice and the rest of the chicken stock to the pork chops and spices, mix well, cover and let sit until the rice soaks up most of the liquid.

Serve the pork chop on one side of the dish, the rice and beans on the other and garnish the rice and beans with strips of roasted red pepper.

Garlic, Wine and Olive Oil

$\mathcal{R}$ICE TRAVELED from the south to the northern Italic peninsula around the fifteenth century. Historians speculate that rice production was decreed by one of the many Dukes during the time of the great northern Italic shipping, trading and cultural influence over Europe. Once a vast Etruscan vineyard site that was wiped out by Celtic warriors in 500 BC, the Po Valley became the center for rice production during the Renaissance.

Today, more than half the world's population consumes rice as a dietary staple, and Italy produces more rice than any Western European country. The most famous of the Italian rice varieties in the United States is the Arborio used to make risotto.

Risotto takes a great amount of time to prepare; its preparation is similar to that of paella, a dish common in parts of Spain. Yet, a fine Arborio dish can be prepared in minutes and it is as good as any risotto that has been slaved over for hours.

INGREDIENTS TO SERVE TWO
3 cloves garlic, chopped
1 shallot, chopped
2 tbl. olive oil
1 cup Arborio rice
2½ quarts of water
1¼ cup chicken stock
⅓ cup dry Marsala
1 large portabello mushroom cap, chopped into ½ inch cubes
handful of pine nuts
2 large sweet roasted red peppers
2 tsp. each of chopped basil, thyme and rosemary leaves
¼ cup chopped parsley
⅔ cup freshly grated Reggiano cheese
ground black pepper to taste

Sauté shallot in olive oil in a large pan or casserole on medium heat until it is translucent; than add the garlic and sauté 30 seconds.

Add to the garlic and shallot the Marsala, 1 cup of chicken stock, 1 tsp. each basil and thyme, 2 tsp. rosemary and the mushroom. Cover and simmer on low flame.

Bring the water to a boil and add the rice (as if you are cooking pasta). Let the water boil again and after five minutes check for consistency; you want the rice firm. Drain the water and add the rice to the mushroom in the pan, cover and let the rice soak up the liquid—check constantly to make sure that the liquid does not dry completely.

Put the pine nuts in a small no-stick pan and toast over high flame, constantly agitating the pan until the nuts turn slightly brown. Immediately add the pine nuts and the rest of the stock to the rice and mushroom and mix everything well, cover over low flame and let the rice soak up most of the liquid for two or three minutes.

Add the grated cheese. Turn off the flame and mix quickly; then serve into pasta bowls. Make a mound of the rice dish in the middle of the bowl and be sure to add all the remaining liquid. Add ground pepper to taste.

Cut the skinned roasted peppers into strips. Line the pepper strips around the rice dish making a spoke arrangement. Garnish with parsley and the remaining basil and thyme in the center of the mound.

Asparagus, smoked seafoods, shellfish or sausages all make wonderful alternatives to the mushroom.

Garlic, Wine and Olive Oil

*M*Y NEIGHBOR, RALPH, died of a heart attack in the mid-1960s; soon after, old man Anton died too. With their deaths, and the deaths of many other old-timers, went backyard gardening, painstaking quality food preparation and vibrant, powerful homemade wines. I grew older too, and the time had arrived for me to make my way into the world.

Her first question, after I announced to my mother that I was getting my own apartment, represented what I thought was alarming reserve: "Who will cook for you?" Then, in a voice laced with dejection, she said, "Don't think you can come here anytime you need a good meal."

My mother was bluffing of course. She gladly fed me whenever I needed a good meal, yet her words were a challenge to me. I wanted to prove that at nineteen I could be on my own, which meant I had to cook for myself. So in 1964, I fired up my first stove in my first apartment. It was in a brownstone one block off of Brooklyn's famous Prospect Park. The tiny stove fit snugly into an alcove the landlord creatively called a kitchen. The refrigerator sat dangerously close to the stove. In my one room, perhaps 10 x 13, I cooked, ate, slept, watched television, listened to music and practiced piano; the bathroom was in the hall, and I shared it—never simultaneously—with two young ladies who lived in the studio apartment next door.

In the 1960s supermarket chains threatened the butcher, baker, produce stand and small grocer. By the standards of thirty years ago, the first supermarket I saw was indeed large. Standing at the precipice of the revolution in shopping, I went to that store to fill up my first refrigerator. The experience filled me with wonder, not only because of the store size and its abundant supply of meats, produce and staples, but because of a discovery about my mother I made on this my first solo-shopping trip.

In those days bottles were still made of glass and the question "plastic or paper?" had yet to become part of the vernacular. It is hard to believe, but lightweight plastic shopping bags with handles didn't exist. The paper bags I carried away from the store were sturdier than the fragile, recycled paper used for bags today, but even sturdy bags split once in a while, especially when over-stuffed with a week or two worth of cans and bottles. It was hard enough for me to juggle the bags on my arms and shoulders, as the weight of their ingredients shifted with every step I took as I struggled to walk the two long city blocks home. But when a bag tore open from the weight of a shifting bottle or can, the task was insurmountable. How, I wondered, did my mother manage to shop like this every day for most of her adult life? I limited my shopping to twice a month.

Out on my own I emulated my mother's cooking and the cooking of my relatives, which meant lots of pasta in tomato sauce; it was all I could do at the time. But I did want to experiment and to learn. One of my first experimental meals was crudely breaded veal cutlet, and a side order of broccoli in garlic and olive oil. The veal cutlet was forgettable; the broccoli was an awakening. I had prepared the broccoli as I remembered my mother doing it—a simple dish of the top two-thirds of the broccoli sautéed in garlic, olive oil and lemon.

INGREDIENTS TO SERVE TWO
3 cloves garlic, chopped
broccoli heads to feed two (the upper three or so inches of the broccoli).
4 tbl. olive oil
1 lemon

Cover the bottom of a cast iron skillet with the oil and add the broccoli. Slice the lemon in four parts. Hold a lemon quarter over your hand above the broccoli in the pot. Squeeze the lemon so that the juice runs through your fingers as you catch the pits in your hand. Do the same with another lemon quarter, and then put the lemon peels into the pan. Cover and simmer (low heat) for about fifteen minutes or until a fork slips with slight resistance into the broccoli. Add the garlic and sauté for 1 minute.

Serve as a side dish, on a plate with a lemon wedge.

I have since learned to make veal cutlet.

INGREDIENTS TO SERVE TWO
3 cloves garlic, minced
4 tbl. olive oil
2 thinly sliced veal cutlets (¼ to ½ pound each)
½ cup plain, dry breadcrumbs
½ cup of milk
1 egg
¼ cup dry Marsala
1 tbl. each chopped basil and oregano
¼ cup freshly grated Romano cheese
ground black pepper to taste
¼ cup chopped parsley
2 lemon wedges

Make sure the veal is nearly paper-thin. Pounding is also necessary; then cover the veal with milk in a bowl, plus the garlic, and refrigerate a few hours.

At dinnertime, remove the veal from the milk and pat it dry. Mix about 1 tsp. of milk with the egg and beat with a fork, mixing it up nicely.

Sauté the garlic, in 2 tbl. olive oil for one minute.

Dip the veal, one cutlet at a time in the egg and milk, let drip and then coat on all sides in the breadcrumb.

Add the rest of the olive oil to the pan and cook the veal on one side until it is golden; repeat on the other side, flipping with a flat spatula. Spread the basil and oregano over the veal and serve in plates.

Deglaze the pan with Marsala; let it simmer until the wine reduces to half, then spoon out the remaining juice over the veal.

Serve with a parsley and Romano cheese garnish and ground black pepper to taste, plus a lemon wedge on the side.

Chicken breast can also be prepared in this style, provided they are sliced not to thick. Instead of the milk, marinade the chicken breast in fresh lemon juice and garlic and let rest a few hours in the refrigerator.

TWO VIEWS OF FLORENCE, ITALY

Garlic, Wine and Olive Oil

—10—

Reversing Course

*A*T NINETEEN, I spent a small portion of my meager paycheck on premium table wines. Neither flush with cash nor smart enough to get a hold of cookbooks, much of what I did in my hole-in-the-wall kitchen was emulation and experimentation—and mostly Italian-oriented.

I also dreamed of exploring Italy, to understand better my place as a descendant of the ancient Mediterranean, and my growing love for cooking. I held that dream for ten years before the means and the opportunity came my way, and when it did I learned a little more than I expected.

Our first trip to Italy began for Anne and me on a train late one night in Amsterdam. The train dropped us off in Munich early the next morning for a layover before moving on to Florence. We were hungry for breakfast and all we could find at the Munich train station at seven o'clock in the morning was potato salad, würst and beer; we passed on the last item.

We also got in a quick walking tour of Munich on that crisp winter day. It was nearing Christmas. Many locals were out shopping and gazing at the decorated shop windows that lined the square in the center of the city, so we joined them. To keep warm, we walked and we ate. We munched on chocolates melted and shaped before our eyes from a pushcart on the square, and we lunched at an outdoor würst stand where we discovered a particular delicacy of Munich, leberkasse (liver-cheese) with mustard and good German beer. After lunch, we sipped warming schnapps in a small café and shopped for leberkasse, bread and wine to take with us on the train to Florence that evening.

Sometime in the night we were bound for Italy, and would have gotten into Florence early the next morning had the Italian railroad workers not gone on strike. The trip came to a complete halt a few miles outside of Florence.

While we waited for the strike to end, I went into a trance. For me, the excitement of finally making it to the motherland and then having to be stuck on the train bordered on the unbearable. I had spent most of my life in Brooklyn, soaking up what culture I could from my heritage. I had known some of the grandparents in the neighborhood who had come from the Old World; I had listened to their dialect, heard their music and, more importantly, eaten their foods. I had been blessed with an Italian temperament and now I was about to see how I would fit in the original place. As time passed, and I looked out the window of the train, I could feel my pulse quicken. It was only a railroad yard, but it was on Italian soil, and it seemed like the first railroad yard in the world. It was only a railroad sign, but because it was written in Italian I thought it was the prettiest railroad sign in the world: Firenze—I said it over and over. Untold hours later, the strike ended.

It was nearing dinnertime in Florence by the time we had checked into a pensione. We ventured outside for a walk through the serenely beautiful Renaissance city which looked more beautiful to us in the fading sunlight, with a golden ray of sunlight dispersed by a mist that muted and softened the copper domes and tiled roofs of the city. On our way to find a restaurant I swooned to an overwhelming sensation: the people around us looked, walked and acted like the people in my neighborhood. They used the same hand gestures, they made the same facial expressions to make a point—they looked like me! My sense of excitement on the train came back in full force. As we walked the fifteenth-century streets I began to feel like I had come home. I was lifted into the clouds where I remained throughout dinner and the rest of the night, and I expected to be there for the rest of the trip. But at lunchtime the following day an Italian waiter grounded me.

Lunch began with a spectacular serving of ravioli en brodo, which on my block was pronounced iraviol en obrod, and which Anne tasted for the first time and fell instantly in love. The dish of pasta in broth symbolizes both simplicity and elegance; no individual flavor overpowers another, not even the generous helping of garlic. We followed the broth with some light "prosciutto con meloni et formaggi" (thin-sliced smoked ham with melons and some cheeses) and a serving of "insalate" (a green salad). Of course, we washed down the meal with the neighborhood wine: Chianti Riserva from Siena, at about five dollars a bottle.

It was Italy, so lingering over lunch for a few hours was expected. Soon we needed to remedy our after-lunch lethargy if we wanted to make that visit to see Michelangelo's *David*. A coffee boost was in order.

The coffee-drinking custom in Brooklyn was to add to a demitasse cup of espresso a twist of lemon peel and a dash of anisette, an anise-flavored liqueur similar to the ouzo in Greece. To Anne, coffee was, well, coffee. She was as unfamiliar with espresso as I was with American cheese. I commissioned the waiter. "Signore, due espressi con anisette, per favore."

It took some doing to persuade the waiter that, despite my American nationality, I was neither stupid nor crazy. What I was, however, was ignorant of the fact that customs in Italy are not widespread—in spirit, the country remains a confederation of mini principalities. Italian customs vary from region to region, town to town, village to village, and house to house. Anisette in coffee is a southern Italian custom, and it is not at all certain that the custom wasn't invented in Brooklyn rather than in southern Italy. (I have since learned that lemon peel was added by the old timers who came to America to satisfy their taste for the slightly bitter coffee they were used to in Sicily.) Even if it were true that the custom of adding lemon and anisette were of southern Italian origin, Anne and I were dining in urbane Tuscany; people in that part of Italy do not relish being confused with the peasants of the Mezzogiorno.

Chastised, we drank our espresso the way the waiter served it— dark, devoid of extra ingredients and just about half full in the tiny cup. In an attempt to have my cup of espresso filled, the next time we ordered espresso in a restaurant I asked for a "doppio" (double). The coffee came in a larger cup, still filled just about half way.

Our most recent visit to Italy's Northeast, to the Veneto and Friuli-Venezia-Giulia regions, bears witness to the fact that customs in Italy remain a local phenomenon.

Unlike Tuscany, where ravioli is common, the most common "en brodo" in the Northeast is tortellini—cheese or meat-stuffed—and the stock used to make the broth in Friuli is from veal. And as we learned in Florence a long time ago, coffee-drinking in Italy, though a widespread custom, still varies from place to place.

The tiny, but uncommonly serene town of Asolo was cut out in a valley bordered to the north by small pastoral hills leading to Asiago, and to the south by a series of roads, the most important being the Roman-built Via Aurelia leading to Padua. Asolo came under Venetian control in the early fourteenth century, having been taken from the Austrian Empire. In the fifteenth century, Venice compensated Caterina Cornaro, queen of Cyprus, with Asolo, for the loss to Venice of the island she inherited from her Cypriot husband's death. (Soon after Cyprus fell, however, its once popular sweet wines had fallen from grace, the trade of sweet wine having been taken over by Portugal and Spain.)

In the late nineteenth century many wealthy people and artists from Britain settled in Asolo, including the poet Robert Browning. Later, after the town had become an artists community, the singer Eleanora Duse made it her home. Today, it is a small, quiet tourist town of incredible beauty, in a valley where fog settles over the head of the Venetian Lion in the square and where stillness reigns.

Anne and I toured the city, including a trip to the top of Caterina Cornaro's castle. Afterwards we lunched in a family restaurant called Cornaro—first, tortellini en brodo for two, and then pasta carbonara with salmon for me, pasta with the flavorful, tiny Italian clams called vongole for Anne, and a half liter of a fine wine for us to share.

For coffee it was cappuccino for Anne, "espresso-doppio" for me. The former was of course supposed to include foamy milk, and it did, but the latter, surprisingly, came with a spot of milk, for that is the way they take their coffee in the family that operates that particular restaurant in that particularly marvelous town.

Garlic, Wine and Olive Oil

RAVIOLI OR TORTELLINI EN BRODO TO SERVE TWO

INGREDIENTS
3 cloves garlic, chopped
2 tbl. olive oil, plus a few drops of oil for the pasta
1 large shallot, chopped
2 carrots, diced
half a head of escarole
1 quart chicken or veal stock
½ cup Marsala
1 tbl. each chopped basil, rosemary and parsley
twenty medium-sized cheese or meat-filled ravioli or tortellini
½ a lemon (for the pasta water)
½ cup freshly grated Reggiano cheese
ground black pepper to taste

Sauté the shallot and carrots in 2 tablespoons olive oil in a large pan until the shallots are translucent; then add the garlic and sauté 30 seconds.

Wash and pat dry the escarole, chop it into small pieces and add it, the basil and the rest of the olive oil to the pan. Sauté for about five minutes, turning the escarole a couple of times, then add the stock and the wine, cover and let simmer (low heat) for at least twenty minutes.

Boil the water for the pasta, adding a few drops of olive oil to prevent sticking plus juice of half a lemon to replace using salt; cook for about ten minutes; strain; then serve the pasta in a soup bowl and pour the broth over it. Add ground black pepper to taste, chopped parsley and grated cheese garnish.

To serve as an appetizer, all you need are a couple of ravioli or tortellini for each dish. But with a chunk of good country bread, this dish makes a wonderfully light dinner.

PART V

To Your Health

The Food Pyramid

small amount of fats, oils, sweets and alcohol

2–3 servings dairy   2–3 servings fish, meat, poultry, beans, eggs

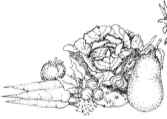

3–5 servings vegetables   2–4 servings fruit

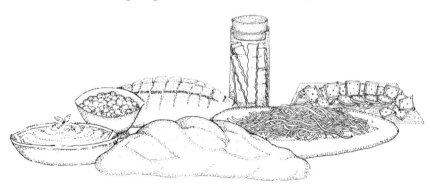

6–11 servings rice, grains, bread, pasta

Garlic, Wine and Olive Oil

−11−

Growing and Consuming for Your Health

*I*T HAS BEEN QUITE A JOURNEY, the food history of civilization that began in the ancient Mesopotamian city of Ur and ultimately funneled its wide past into the narrow streets of Brooklyn, New York.

My passport says I am an American citizen, but my ancestry marks me a Mediterranean, as do my temperament, spirit and culinary taste. I am forever fascinated by the story of the convergence of garlic, wine and olive oil in the Mediterranean region, and I am pleased that "my people" played a role in bringing the three foods to America. Since my first journey to Italy in 1975 I have returned twice to attend the annual major wine show, VinItaly, and to tour the north. I plan a reverse journey in the near future, to arrive on Italy's shores not as a brief visitor but as a long-term resident. The beaming eyes, ruddy smiles and enfolding arms each time I visit Italy, overwhelm and beckon me. It is no accident that these warm Mediterranean traits explode at the lunch or dinner table, for that is where Italians are most alive and comfortable, and that is where they exhibit their uncommonly healthy passion for life. But until my next trip to Italy, I have memories and recipes, and I am safe in the knowledge that Americans can equally benefit in ready access to Mediterranean foods. In fact, there are scientists who say that we should take full advantage of that access—for our health.

Modern science offers numerous studies that point to what it is that gives Mediterraneans a healthy edge over other Western peoples. It seems Mediterraneans are what they eat, and it comes as no surprise to me to discover the healthy role that science ascribes to garlic, wine and olive oil. Perhaps it is good to review a sampling of the data.

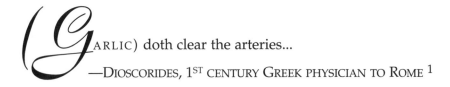

(GARLIC) doth clear the arteries...

—DIOSCORIDES, 1ST CENTURY GREEK PHYSICIAN TO ROME [1]

AT THE END OF THE NINETEENTH CENTURY scientists began to document what thousands of years of ancient wisdom said about garlic. The great bacteria researcher, Louis Pasteur, played a role in these scientific discoveries, when in 1858, he wrote of garlic's antiseptic capacity. In the early part of the twentieth century, picking up on the bacteria research that had been done, tests carried out by an army doctor on the Eastern front led to Allisatin, a pharmaceutical pill that contained an active ingredient in garlic: allicin. Since then, scientists have presented numerous studies showing the bactericidal nature of allicin (allicin is sold in Russia as an antibiotic). Allicin is a natural chemical reaction that occurs when two chemicals found in garlic—alliin and allinase—are blended by crushing or cutting a garlic clove.

In the 1970s Japanese scientists found that when mixed with garlic, vitamin B1 (thiamin) is more readily assimilated in the normally B1 resistant intestinal tract of the human body. These studies led to dietary supplements to combine garlic and B1 to rectify a common vitamin deficiency in Japan. The Japanese also claim the chemical, germanium, which they found in garlic, is an anti-cancer specific.

The Garlic Information Center, a section of the nutrition department at New York Hospital-Cornell University Medical Center, in New York City, agrees with the many beneficial health findings attributed to garlic. As part of the nutrition department, the information center offers a table listing the benefits of garlic suggested by various available scientific literature. To locate the Garlic Information Center on the Internet, go to www.garlic-page.com/health.html; they list a phone number: 212-327-7707.

According to the Garlic Information Center, a daily diet of garlic is believed to protect the heart, enhance the immune system, protect the nervous system, act as an anti-microbial agent, possibly prevent and treat some forms of cancer and protect the body from toxins. Garlic is considered an antioxidant. It acts on free radicals connected to heart disease, as well as to the aging process. Garlic is also under study for its possible ability to lower blood sugar levels (good for diabetics) and as an anti-arthritic.

Garlic appears to benefit us because it lowers blood cholesterol, lowers blood triglycerides, thins the blood to increase circulation and lowers high blood pressure. The people at Cornell also say that garlic might help fight cold and flu as well as infections. What's more, candida, a yeast that attacks parts of the human body, has been killed in test tubes where garlic was introduced, and numerous laboratory tests show that garlic kills certain other bacteria.

The Center states that studies with animals show that garlic inhibits cancer causing compounds, preventing them from binding to DNA, and it decreases side effects of cancer drug therapies such as damage from radiation; in that vein, Italian and Chinese scientists have correlated heavy garlic use with decreased risk of stomach cancer.

In medieval times it was popular for physician monks to treat lepers and other patients with whole, raw garlic. But according to the Garlic Information Center, scientists and nutritionists warn against eating raw garlic—it can hurt the lining of the intestines and it can pass along its own microbial contaminants picked up from the soil in which it was grown. Scientists recommend aging garlic to reduce its potential side effects, which are mostly gastrointestinal-related, and then cooking it prior to consumption.

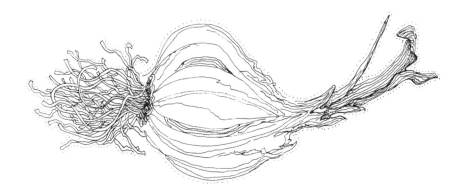

*T*O BE CERTAIN of garlic's freshness and quality, it is best to grow it yourself.

*G*ARLIC IS AN EASY GARDEN PLANT, provided you do a few simple things. First, locate your nearest garlic festival or farmers market. This is where you should find the best seed garlic to start your garden. There are many varieties of garlic, so you should find out from the farmer and from your own experiments which will best suit your site and your taste. If you plant enough garlic, you then can put aside some of the bulbs you reap to seed the next crop.

Garlic likes crumbly, moist—but not muddy—earth and a good degree of organic matter like compost, which should be added to the soil yearly. Clay soils make harvesting hard work. Clay also retains water and sometimes requires thinning out with garden-grade sand in order for garlic to grow properly. Generally, minimal care in good soil produces fabulous garlic, and many garlic growers are convinced that when you seed with your own garlic the plants become increasingly stronger, developing a kind of genetic link to their specific site.

Like ornamental bulbs, garlic is planted in autumn, each clove three to five inches apart, upright, and no more than an inch deep. The rows should be separated by about 12 inches, for soil cultivation. The bulbs should be insulated with compost or dead leaves so that a winter warm spell prevents them from sprouting or protects them if they do sprout and the weather turns cold again.

In the spring, and during the growing season, keep the plants moist but not soaked. In July be on the lookout for the topset or scape—a bulb-like flower that is at the top of a thick stalk that appears from the middle of the plant. In most cases, removal of the flower produces larger bulbs underground. Let the loop of the stalk uncurl and straighten up beyond a 45 degree angle before you remove the scape.

It is time to pick garlic when most of the leaves turn brown and die back from the bottom. Some leaves—four or five—should remain mostly green; these are the "wrappers" for the picked bulb. Picking takes place in late July. Sometimes, as in the oppressively hot Northeastern summer of 1999, picking is early. That year, picking was so early that many of the scapes never got removed.

The best way to dig up garlic is to insert a digging tool a couple of inches from the stalk, dig a half circle and then push into the soil to get under the bulb. While holding the base of the stalk, simultaneously pull the stalk (lightly) and push up from under the bulb.

Rinse and separate the plants and lie them out to dry—a rock or flat platform is good—but not in direct sunlight. Clip the roots (beard) to halt moisture collection and then clip the tops within an inch of the bulb, or tie the bulbs together by braiding the stalks.

Cloves that have been damaged during picking will cause the bulb to rot. If you can dry and preserve the bulb for a couple of weeks before rot sets in, you should cook with the good cloves right away.

Never refrigerate garlic. It will store for about half a year provided the temperature is between 32 and 40 degrees Fahrenheit and humidity is low. A nicely decorative way to store homegrown garlic is to hang braided stalks in a cool, dry place, pulling a bulb from the stalk each time you need to use one.

Mostly Garlic, a quarterly periodical, is filled with growing, cooking, health and historical facts about garlic. To subscribe online go to www.mostlygarlic.com.ca, or write to: Mostly Garlic, 19 E. Church Street, Milan, Ohio 44846.

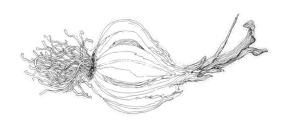

*M*ORTAR THE GARLIC *and boil it in milk, or else beat the garlic and mix it with soft cheese; it is a cure for catarrhs... employed similarly, and taken with peas or beans, (garlic) is good for hoarseness...is found to be more serviceable cooked than raw...is a soporific...and imparts to the body an additional ruddiness...*
—RECIPE FROM PLINY'S *NATURAL HISTORY*, 1ST CENTURY AD [2]

*N*OTICE THE MENTION OF MILK and cheese in Pliny's recipe; it reflects a Roman diet that was heavy in dairy products.

Colman Andrews, in *Flavors of the Riviera,* points out that the volume of cheese and other fats he saw modern-day Mediterraneans consume during his travels seems in conflict with our American concept of the low-fat Mediterranean diet based on grains and vegetables.

Mr. Andrews has a point, but recent scientific findings suggest that Mediterraneans are protected against artery damage, thanks to the great amount of wine they take with their cheese, forming both a taste and symbiotic relationship that few food pairings equal. Yet it is certainly healthier to keep saturated animal fats to a minimum—so says the medical profession and the Federal Government of the United States of America.

The Food and Drug Administration (FDA) has done away with the food chart that was tacked to the cafeteria wall in P.S. 4 when I went to grade school. The old chart (in the form of a triangle) listed five basic food groups for daily consumption: meat, dairy, grain, vegetables and fruits. In the nineteen fifties, neighborhood kids used to wonder if our Italian diet heavy in grains, vegetables, unsaturated oil and wine made us candidates for an appearance at the House Un-American Activities Committee. We can finally breathe a sigh of relief: the federal government vindicates us without hearings, but of course not without controversy.

The new FDA chart both adds to and inverts the old one, listing in order of importance grains, vegetables, fruits, dairy, meats, eggs and legumes, fats, oils and sweets (in the form of a pyramid). The chart is accompanied by written Dietary Guidelines that some refer to as "The Mediterranean Diet." (If the ancients were to step out of a time machine they would also relate to the chart, especially if they were to recognize the Pyramid that depicts it.) In its Dietary Guidelines the FDA points out the potential benefit of *moderate* alcohol consumption, while at the same time the guidelines contain numerous caveats on the subject of alcohol.

In November, 1997, Oldways Preservation and Exchange Trust, a Boston-based food group with a bent toward healthy dietary alternatives endorsed a vegetarian diet pyramid that also includes alcohol in moderation with meals. This pyramid is built around vegetables, fruits, whole grains and legumes.

Government being what it is, however, the FDA chart presents us with a dilemma: the view of wine today at one branch of government, FDA, contradicts the view held at another branch of government, the Bureau of Alcohol, Tobacco and Firearms (BATF).

The BATF is responsible for regulating and collecting federal excise taxes from wine producers, and also for interpreting alcohol control policy. The organization's narrow interpretation of laws prohibits alcoholic beverage producers from imparting information regarding scientifically proven beneficial health effects connected to moderate alcohol consumption. So you will not hear wine producers say that moderate wine consumption might be good for you, but the BATF cannot stop others from reporting the news.

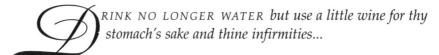

RINK NO LONGER WATER but use a little wine for thy stomach's sake and thine infirmities...

—1 TIMOTHY 5:23

*O*NCE AGAIN, Louis Pasteur was in the vanguard, this time when he proclaimed wine the most healthful drink. His seminal work with bacteria included the discovery that wine is altered by the different bacteria with which it comes into contact during its life cycle as a grape on the vine, as a juice in fermentation and as a wine in storage. Pasteur's discoveries are responsible, both directly and indirectly, for much of the way table wine is produced. Winemaking is today less a profession of chance than it once was. With what winemakers know about bacteria, and how to control them, it is rare when a wine that has turned bad appears on the market, which is not to be confused with a bad wine—one that has not been made well. Since Pasteur, many components that make up wine have been isolated, some of which modern science is only beginning to understand.

In the early 1990s, in a segment for CBS Television News, Sixty Minutes correspondent, Morley Safer, presented a report called The French Paradox. The "paradox" refers to evidence that, while they eat as much, or more, saturated animal fats than Americans do, the French suffer significantly fewer deaths, per capita, from coronary disease. The major difference between the two diets, according to those who discovered the paradox, is that the French drink lots of red wine with their meals. The United States has a dismally low per capita annual wine consumption among industrial nations and at the same time, our country enjoys the highest rates of death from coronary disease among all nations. A parallel?

Over the years, scientific data presented by Harvard Medical School and The American Cancer Society in the 1980s, plus the National Institute on Alcohol and the American Heart Association in 1996, to name a few research organizations, indicate that a diet that includes moderate alcohol consumption can be beneficial to our health, especially to our heart. The Wine Institute, in California, provides information about these health studies at their Internet site: www.wineinstitute.org.

The many studies indicate that alcohol increases levels of high-density lipoproteins (HDL) in our blood. HDLs transport cholesterol from the blood to the liver where it is altered and/or destroyed. This is commonly known as the good cholesterol activity.

The bad cholesterol activity happens when low density lipoproteins (LDL). transport cholesterol away from the liver, dumping it into tissues, including the walls of arteries where cholesterol builds and clogs up.

In a study a few years ago, at Queen Elizabeth Hospital in Birmingham, England, red wine was discovered to be an antioxidant. The news was not surprising to winemakers.

Wine is not just alcohol; it is a complex beverage that consists of trace nutrients and many phenolic compounds. Two phenolics in wine—quercetin and rutin—are antioxidants. Scientists say antioxidants slow down the aging process. Coincidentally, low density lipoprotein (the bad cholesterol LDL) is prone to damaging oxidation, and it could also benefit from the action of antioxidants; this is why scientists believe that vitamin E, garlic and now wine are important to the diet.

In 1997, researchers at Cornell University, Ithaca, New York, isolated a chemical in wine, resveratrol, which not only appears to protect against heart disease, but also is indicated as an anti-cancer agent.

Resveratrol resides in all grape skins but is found in higher concentrations in grape crops that are subjected to extensive fungal attacks in the vineyard—the grapes produce resveratrol as a natural response against disease. The heating effect of fermentation apparently leaches resveratrol from grape skins and into the wine. Beneficial concentrations of resveratrol are found mainly in red wine because, unlike white wine, which is first pressed into juice and then often subjected to cool fermentation, red wine is fermented on the skins, often getting quite warm in the process, before it is pressed into wine.

Some of the healthy components in grapes have been packaged. Health food stores and health food sections in large supermarkets carry tablets of quercetin and rutin. In addition, there is something on the market called wine grape extract. A recent analysis of grape extract pills done at Cornell University, however, showed that it could take a dozen or more pills a day to get the health benefit found in one glass of wine.

Protection from heart disease, and perhaps cancer, are the main health benefits connected to daily moderate wine consumption, and that is no small matter. Wine also contains beneficial trace elements. And wine contains enough acidity to kill off some potential harmful bacteria from spoiled food, the same acidity that also helps to stimulate saliva which, in turn, helps in digestion.

St. Paul must have known something about wine when he recommended that Timothy take "a little wine..." The question is: what is a little, or what is moderation?

WINE IS LIKE LIFE TO MEN, if you drink it in moderation.
                                                              —Ecclesiastes 31:27

READ THE GOVERNMENT WARNING on wine labels and you would think the stuff is bad for you—period. As we see, however, new evidence about alcohol consumption seems to point in the opposite direction, provided those who consume it do so with moderation. And when we speak of moderation in wine consumption, we have none other than Louis Pasteur to look to for guidance. He recommended daily wine intake of about 375 milliliters; that happens to equal half the contents of a standard 750 ml. bottle of table wine, and it is close to the daily table wine consumption recommended today for most. ("Table wine" is a legally defined term that refers to wine of anywhere from roughly eight to fifteen percent alcohol by volume.)

A five ounce glass of table wine, at twelve percent alcohol by volume, provides approximately the same amount of alcohol as twelve ounces of beer or one shot of whiskey. For the average healthy male or female, moderate wine consumption is anywhere from one to three glasses of wine per day. As for calories, that glass of wine hovers at 100.

For the purposes of simplicity, the effect of alcohol abuse appears to begin where moderation leaves off.

𝒴OU CAN GROW your own winegrapes in a home garden, but to succeed you need to know a few things.

Cultivated grapevines are the result of hundreds of crossbred vines worked on over multiple centuries. If you plant grapevine seeds, the plant reverts to any number of crosses in its lineage. Also, grapevines have been bred to resist certain diseases. So to be sure you get the grape variety you seek, with a genetic means toward resisting the most serious diseases, you must plant young vines that have been grafted onto a particular rootstock. The two important sources of nursery-grafted vines are California and New York state. But before you drop a load of cash on a few dozen vines you should learn which grape varieties and which rootstock clone will flourish in your soil and climate.

To find out which winegrapes can survive best in your area, and which grapes will grow to give you the benefit of their flavor characteristics, visit your nearest agricultural cooperative extension office. Most universities, especially those in heavy agricultural communities, have such an office, and those that do not can certainly direct you to where you can find the information.

When you are ready to plant vines remember: it takes about 200 pounds of grapes to produce about 15 gallons of filtered and finished wine. So find out what the optimum yield is for each grape variety, and decide how much wine you want to make before you plant.

You must read and learn how to tend vines or face regular failure growing grapes. Optimum fruit production depends on many factors, not the least of which is how and when the vines are pruned. In fact, growing grapes is a four-season endeavor; work must be performed even when the vines are dormant.

When you are ready to make wine, you need a few books on that subject too (for a brief list, see the appendix). Luckily, the market offers every kind of equipment needed to make wine on a small scale. Find your nearest home winemaking supplier and form a relationship. Most people who make and sell winemaking equipment are helpful and sharing. If you live in an apartment, or you aren't the grape growing type, you can hook up with a reputable home winemaking operation that supplies either grapes, grape juice or grape concentrate, or a combination of any of the three.

One of the better ways to make the right connections for home winemaking is to join the American Wine Society, 3006 Latta Road, Rochester, New York 14612-3298.

WINE THAT MAKETH GLAD the heart of man, and oil to make his face shine.

—PSALMS 104:15

CERTAIN FATS ARE ESSENTIAL in the human diet—the unsaturated kind. Olive oil is monounsaturated; it provides essential unsaturated and polyunsaturated fats. (I have read that some olive oil contains about 10% saturated fat, but the statement did not identify which of the oils do. My suspicion is those are lesser olive oils blended with some other oil.)

When they look to the three great olive oil-producing nations—Spain, Italy and Greece—scientists find low rates of heart disease, partly, we are told, because olive oil gives citizens of those countries extra protection against artery hardening. But olive oil offers a lot more than unsaturated fats: it is easily digested, quickly absorbed, includes trace components like chlorophyll, stimulates appetite and does not turn rancid after cooking. A tablespoon of olive oil (about 10 grams) includes 9mg of vitamin E and 100g of vitamin A. Olive oil contains no carbohydrates, no sodium and, of course, no cholesterol. The news is all good—well, not quite. That tablespoonful of olive oil comes with about 100 calories, all from fat. Like other oils, olive oil can be fattening.

Unfortunately, a comprehensive olive oil Web site on the Internet is difficult to locate, but there are many sites concerning the olive provided by olive oil membership councils as well as private companies. Just type in "olive oil" on your search engine. The European-based International Olive Oil Council operates a hotline: 800-232-6548, which provides mainly recipes and a list of nutritionists.

Just as it was when Cato said it, the best olive oil is cold pressed *extra virgin*. This oil comes with less than 1 percent acidity, and is made of first-choice olives. One step down the olive oil quality scale is called *virgin*. These oils are often blended with highly refined olive oils to reduce acidity and cost; they are normally cold pressed. Hot pressing, or introducing hot water to the pressing process can diminish the oil's quality, which leads to the next level of olive oil. An olive oil product labeled *pure* exemplifies the success of marketing over information; this product is often nothing more than pulp that is hard-pressed after the best oil has been taken off. The resulting oil is subject to high temperatures, and solvents are used in the process.

The watchdog North American Olive Oil Association claims to rigorously test olive oils found in supermarkets to assure accuracy in labeling, but it has little chance of doing the same in the widely scattered restaurant trade. Yet the organization did come across a problem brought to their attention by restaurateurs who believed the price for olive oil they were quoted was too good to be true. Some packer/distributors sold a product labeled Olive Pomace Brand. The product was supposed to have been from Italy but was actually blended on the West Coast of the United States. Even worse, it contained no trace of olive oil—it was canola oil.

The email address for the North American Olive Oil Association is naooa@afius.org; their phone number is 732-583-8188.

You can find products in supermarkets such as Olive Pomace Oil. Even if they are really from olives, I am told these oils are made from the worse part of the olive (even from crushed olive pits) to produce the worse possible taste. But these products might serve some purpose after all. A recent study at Harvard School of Public Health discovered that olive oil kills head lice by smothering their breathing. According to the report, olive oil also makes nit removal easy and it re-moisturizes the scalp, something that cannot be said for the prescription medicine used to kill head lice. Also, according to the study, olive oil offers no potential health hazards to a child, something again that cannot be said for the prescription drugs.

It is best to store your cooking olive oil in an airtight container, in a dark, cool cupboard. If stored this way, it should last a year. Refrigeration is not necessary and in fact clouds uncooked olive oil.

The antioxidant qualities of olive oil that help to slow down the aging process in us also serve to keep the oil stable at high cooking temperatures. Since olive oil does not turn rancid after it has been cooked, you can filter particles left behind with a fine filter and then you can refrigerate and re-use the oil as much as ten times; this is the only time you should refrigerate olive oil.

Olives are inedible until their natural glucocides have been drawn out. To do this, they must be cured, and there are a number of ways to do that. Some olives are soaked in oil or water for many months. Other olives face up to six months in salt-brine or many months in dry salt. Another olive cure uses an alkaline wash like soda ash. The brine and salt cured olives most available to us in supermarkets fare better when served, sparingly, in salads or as puréed appetizers mixed with spices.

Illustration by Tina Howe

Garlic, Wine and Olive Oil

*O*LIVE TREES, LIKE GRAPEVINES, should not be started from seed. If the tree is started from seed the plant could revert to its original wild state. So to grow your own olive trees you must first locate a nursery for stock created either from cuttings or grafts. For the family to enjoy olives from the family tree you must have lots of time and plenty of offspring—it takes nearly a generation before a cultivated olive tree produces its best edible crop. But once established, it is nearly impossible to kill olive tree roots, which grow large and knurly as they become saturated with oil. Stories of olive shoots popping up through paved driveways in California are not uncommon, and annual olive shoots in Tunisia, at the site of ancient Carthage, are said to come from roots the Romans failed to burn during their pillage of Carthage in 146 BC. Suffice to say, when handled properly olive trees provide quality fruit and oil for generations.

Olive trees need lots of sun and well-drained soil in a location where winter temperatures fall to no less than 15 degrees Fahrenheit, and where there is little chance for late spring frosts, which leaves out a great part of North America.

The expensive equipment necessary to make olive oil plus the amount of hard work it takes—one tree will give you perhaps one liter of oil—ensure that even if you live in the right place, and you prune and care for your olive tree, and you have all the time and generations necessary to be there for its first crop, you still will have to buy commercial olive oil.

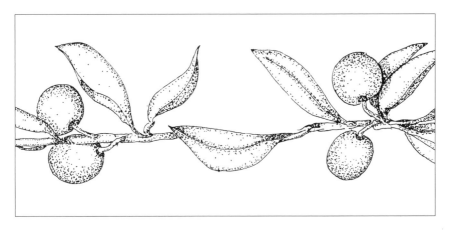

PART VI

Personal Recipe Favorites

−12−

Mangiare

O PARAPHRASE A WRITER I once read in the *New Yorker*— add a little garlic here or pepper there to an existing recipe and the recipe becomes yours. He told the story of a friend who gave a dinner party at which a journalist guest asked him for the recipe to the main course. The friend thought no more of the journalist's request until later when he read the recipe in a cookbook crediting him for the dish. The problem was he got the recipe from another friend, a respected American chef and cookbook writer. When the man apologized for the situation, the venerable chef said it was okay because, "I got the recipe from someone else."

The ancient recipes in this book, plus some of the old but not necessarily ancient recipes, are the result of my research, the resources for which are cited with footnotes. The modern recipes throughout the book, and in this chapter, made their way into my kitchen either through childhood memories, dog-eared cookbooks, dinners at restaurants or at the homes of friends; every recipe has been altered to suit my taste. In fact, I continually alter recipes, adding, subtracting or replacing ingredients as I experiment—forever.

Even those of us who find cooking fun and relaxing often find little time in which to do it; with a few exceptions, the recipes in this book take only a short time to prepare. You will notice, too, except for a particular potato recipe, and the rare times I use soy sauce, I add no salt when I cook. That is because I believe that salt interrupts natural flavors, and salt is not a good companion to wine— not to mention the possible health benefits of reducing salt in the diet. I prefer natural spices to bring out or to augment flavors. And although I suggest them in this book, I hardly measure additions of spices, choosing instead to do it by feel.

For spices to truly bring out flavor they must be fresh or as close to it as possible. Some herbs and spices lose their flavor when dried, particularly basil, cilantro and parsley. Many supermarkets sell some of these spices as hothouse-grown, uprooted plants throughout the winter. These plants offer the freshest flavors you can get off-season. Of course, growing spices in the summer garden is preferable.

At the end of the summer growing season, you can preserve spices like basil and oregano by letting bunches of their leaves rest for about a month in a tightly sealed jar filled to the top with olive oil. When the month is up, remove the leaves, run the oil through a fine filter, and you have herbed olive oil to cook with throughout the winter.

My mother-in-law says she has frozen fresh herbs by covering them with water in an ice tray and freezing them. When they are frozen, she places them in freezer bags and stores them. To use the frozen herbs she thaws them, dumps the water and dries the herbs in a salad spinner.

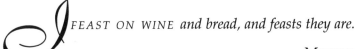 *FEAST ON WINE and bread, and feasts they are.*

—MICHELANGELO 1

A FEW YEARS AGO I read a book by David Rosengarten and Joshua Wesson, *Red Wine With Fish*. In their irreverent presentation, the authors make good points regarding how to pair wine with food. They are less concerned with the color of a wine than its characteristics; is it fruity, hot (alcoholic), soft or crisp (its acidity), spicy or full-bodied (rich on the tongue), and is the swallow clean and short or tannic and lingering? These attributes, in various combinations with one another, make or break wine and food pairings. Of course, a few traditional pairings should go relatively unchallenged. For instance, grilled steak generally requires the richness of a strong red wine and oysters on the half shell would be even more naked without a crisp white wine right beside.

In Mediterranean countries centuries of experience have led the locals to produce the best wines to match local foods. In many cases, when you are in a European wine-producing region you will find little, if any, wine from another wine-producing region. This kind of cultural symbiosis between wine and dinner did not happen overnight, yet there is no mystery to marrying wine with food.

If you are new to wine, it helps to take a class to learn what various wines are supposed to taste like. But do not be afraid to pair recipes with many different wines at home; that is the best and most fun way to learn. Constant tasting is the surest way to develop appreciation.

Each of the following recipes comes with a wine recommendation, except in the case of soup, which receives a blanket wine recommendation. The recipe chapter is followed with an appendix to cross-reference wines with the recipes, and a second appendix to do the reverse. The wine list I offer by no means represents a comprehensive list either of available wines on the market or of all the potentially good pairings of wine and the recipes in this book— they are merely indication of what can be.

Buon apettito!

Thomas Pellechia

Soups

*W*E ALL KNOW how good chicken soup makes us feel when we have a cold or flu. But to prepare good chicken soup, you first need a chicken stock.

*T*HE FOLLOWING SIMPLE CHICKEN STOCK is sans vegetables. Traditional stock calls for carrots and/or celery but you can add those and other vegetables as you need them when you prepare each separate dish that will take chicken stock. This way, you have a relatively clear chicken stock.

INGREDIENTS
4 cloves of garlic, chopped
a few shallots (or handful of scallions or leeks) chopped
1 frying chicken
large pot of water

Thoroughly rinse the chicken, making sure its insides are free of packaged gizzards, and such. Lay the chicken—legs up—in enough water to cover just above the thighs. Add the garlic and shallot to the pot. Cover and bring to a boil, at which time foam will rise to the top. Grab a large spoon, scoop up the foam and discard it. Then turn down the flame to simmer, and cover.

Let the chicken simmer until the legs can be yanked off with ease. When that time arrives, pull the chicken out of the water; be sure to also get out of the water all the chicken scraps that might have fallen off when you lifted the chicken. (A great idea is to use a pasta-cooker—a pot with a large pasta strainer. Put the chicken in the strainer and place the strainer into the pot. After cooking, just lift the strainer, and the chicken, out of the water to cool.)

Some clarify their stock with egg white. It seems an unnecessary step. Simply strain the liquid through a filter or sieve and into 16 or 8-ounce preserving jars for refrigerating; fill to $2/3$ of the jar. The following day, scrape the fat at the top of each jar. You can use the stock right away or if you refrigerate for future use, you must use the stock within three days. The stock can be frozen too. When you freeze, be sure not to tighten the jar lid so that the expansion of the liquid inside does not crack the jar.

Use the meat of the boiled whole chicken in chicken soup or chicken salad.

OTHER SOUP STOCK MATERIAL

VEGETABLE

Save in a bowl juice from cooked or steamed vegetables. Add a couple of dashes of soy sauce to it, refrigerate and use it within a few days, or freeze it. When you want to use it for cooking, you can decide which vegetables you would like to chop and add. Incidentally, I use the light soy sauce with less salt.

VEAL OR BEEF STOCK

Add chopped garlic in enough water to cover a marrow bone or bones and boil until cooked. Put a couple of dashes of Tabasco or soy sauce into it, or both, refrigerate and use within a few days, or freeze.

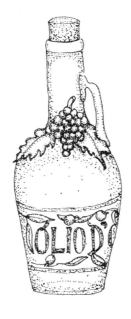

EW WINES STAND UP to the hardiness of the following soups, but the ones that do create a delightful adventure. For a truly satisfying wine and soup experience try a glass of Madeira (Sercial or Verdelho) or dry sherry. For the former, do not be fooled by domestic wines called Madeira—when compared to the real thing from the Portuguese island of the same name, they simply do not make the grade. There are, however, one or two domestic sherries that are good, but they give no particular reason other than price to forego the delightful original from Jerez, Spain.

Garlic, Wine and Olive Oil

CHICKEN SOUP TO SERVE FOUR

INGREDIENTS
12 cloves garlic, pressed
2 tbl. olive oil
the chicken you used to make stock
2 quarts chicken stock
½ cup of either dry Marsala, Madeira or sherry
1 large onion, chopped
2 large carrots, diced small
4 tablespoons chopped parsley
ground black pepper to taste

Warm up the chicken stock.

Sauté the onion and carrots in olive oil for about three minutes; then add the garlic and cook for two more minutes. Deglaze the pan with ¼ cup of wine and let the wine reduce to half. Add all the ingredients, except the pepper, to the stock, cover and simmer for half an hour.

Trim the skin from the chicken and break the meat into small pieces—try to get all the bones out; there is nothing so dangerous and annoying as chicken bones in soup, or in your throat. Add the chicken pieces and the rest of the wine to the pot, stir, cover and simmer for fifteen minutes to half an hour.

Serve in bowls and sprinkle with pepper to taste.

For chicken soup that sticks to your ribs place a ¼-cup of hot, cooked rice in each serving bowl, then ladle the soup over it.

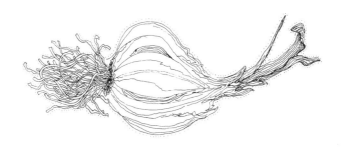

$\mathcal{E}$SCAROLE EN BRODO has been a favorite of mine since I was a child. Without the prosciutto addition it is a cheap and hardy soup.

INGREDIENTS TO SERVE FOUR
4 cloves garlic
2 shallots, chopped
3 carrots, sliced thin
3 tbl. olive oil
head of escarole
¼ pound of prosciutto
2 quarts veal or chicken stock
⅓ cup dry Madeira or sherry
¼ cup each chopped parsley and basil
handful rosemary leaves
½ cup grated Reggiano cheese
ground black pepper to taste

Clean and chop the escarole into small pieces.

In a large pan add the olive oil, garlic, shallot and carrots and on top of them add the escarole. Sauté until the escarole wilts, then add the stock, wine, parsley, basil and rosemary, cover and simmer for half an hour.

Just before serving the soup cut with a meat scissors small pieces of prosciutto; fill the bowls with soup, add small pieces of prosciutto, sprinkle Reggiano and pepper to taste.

Garlic, Wine and Olive Oil

I DO NOT SKI, but my friends used to like it when I joined them at the ski lodge because I would have one of the following two soups ready for their return from the slopes.

LENTIL SOUP
INGREDIENTS TO SERVE FOUR
4 cloves garlic, chopped
1 onion, chopped
3 tbl. olive oil
16 oz. dried lentils
1 veal shank
2 cups chicken stock
½ cup dry Marsala
4 cups water or vegetable stock
½ head of escarole
2 large carrots, diced small
2 medium-sized (red) potatoes, quartered (with skins)
1 tbl. chopped basil
handful chopped parsley
ground black pepper to taste

Clean and soak the lentils in water for an hour or two to soften them while you stew the veal shank in 4 cups water over medium heat in a covered soup pot.

Clean and chop the escarole into small pieces.

In a separate pot, sauté onion in 2 tbl. olive oil until it is translucent, then add remaining olive oil plus the garlic, basil and half of the chopped escarole. Cover and simmer for about five minutes; then turn off the flame.

Add 1 cup chicken stock, lentils, carrots, potatoes and chopped parsley to the veal shank in the soup pot; cover and simmer for fifteen minutes.

Add the rest of the chicken stock, the wine, the rest of the escarole, garlic and basil, mix and cover and simmer for ½ hour. Check to see if you want more liquid. If so, add water, a little at a time. Cover and simmer for another hour.

Serve in a soup bowl. Sprinkle with black pepper to taste.

PEA SOUP

INGREDIENTS TO SERVE FOUR
4 cloves garlic, chopped
1 onion, chopped
2 tbl. olive oil
16 oz. dry split peas
6 cups water or vegetable stock
½ cup dry Marsala
2 large carrots, diced
2 medium-sized red potatoes, quartered (with skins)
2 large celery stalks, chopped
1 ham bone
ground black pepper to taste

Rinse and soak the dried peas for at least a couple of hours.

Sauté the onion in olive oil until it is translucent; then add the garlic and sauté 30 seconds.

Put all ingredients except the pepper into a large soup pot and then add the stock or water plus ⅓ cup of wine.

Cover and simmer for about an hour.

Pea soup is thick and therefore difficult to keep from burning in the pot. Put a grill warmer under the pot to minimize burning, but you must also check and stir every few minutes. If you want more liquid add water or vegetable stock, slowly.

Sprinkle black pepper to taste when serving.

POTATO AND LEEK SOUP

offers a delicate touch and a marvelous sense of sustenance.
INGREDIENTS TO SERVE FOUR
4 cloves garlic, pressed
2 tbl. olive oil
4 cups chicken stock
½ cup dry Marsala
2 quarts water
4 potatoes, cubed (with skins)
4 leeks, chopped
2 tbl. chopped dill

½ cup heavy cream
handful chopped parsley
ground black pepper to taste

Boil the potatoes in 2 quarts of water in a large soup pot until you can easily slip a fork through them; drain and put the potatoes aside. Also, put the heavy cream on the counter to warm it to room temperature.

Sauté the garlic in olive oil in a pan for one minute and then add the leeks, dill and a ½-cup of wine, cover and simmer for five minutes, and then add everything, plus the chicken stock, to a soup pot, cover and simmer for ½ an hour.

Just before serving, add the heavy cream, stir and serve into soup bowls.

Garnish with parsley and sprinkle with pepper.

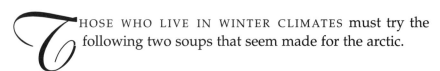 HOSE WHO LIVE IN WINTER CLIMATES must try the following two soups that seem made for the arctic.

PUMPKIN-CURRY SOUP.
PREPARING THE PUMPKIN
Either cook and purée a fresh pumpkin or buy a can of puréed pumpkin—get the kind that includes pumpkin only, no other ingredients.

To cook a pumpkin, first hollow it out and then quarter it (save the seeds to roast later for snacking). Steam, bake or boil the quarters until the pumpkin flesh is soft enough to purée.

INGREDIENTS TO SERVE FOUR:
4 cloves garlic, pressed
1 shallot, chopped
2 tbl. olive oil
1 quart puréed pumpkin
2 large carrots, chopped
1 cup chicken stock
1 cup vegetable stock (plus 1 cup in case you want more)
½ cup dry Marsala

2 tbl. curry powder (plus more, to taste)
a dozen walnuts, shelled and broken into pieces
2 ounces heavy cream
¼ cup chopped parsley

Put the cream on the counter to get it up to room temperature. Sauté the garlic, carrots and shallot in olive oil until the shallots are translucent. Let cool, and then purée together.

Warm the chicken stock in a soup pot.

Add all the vegetables and the pumpkin to the chicken stock and stir vigorously. Add the vegetable stock, slowly, stirring until you get a loose but not watery mixture; if it takes less than 2 cups of vegetable stock, fine, save the rest for another time.

Add the curry and wine, stir and simmer for ten minutes.

Just before serving, turn the flame out under the pot and add the heavy cream to the soup by pouring it into the pot in a circular motion; then stir vigorously and serve.

Garnish with walnuts and chopped parsley.

Incidentally, any squash can replace pumpkin for this recipe; even sweet potato will do.

SUGAR BEET SOUP
INGREDIENTS TO SERVE FOUR
4 cloves garlic, pressed
1 shallot, chopped
2 tbl. olive oil
2 large carrots, diced
8 whole beets
2 tbl. caraway seed
2 cups chicken stock
½ cup dry sherry
either a dollop of sour cream or ½-cup heavy cream
ground black pepper to taste
handful chopped parsley

Cut away the beet greens, which you can steam and enjoy as a side dish. Cut off the root and then peel the skin with a potato peeler. Rinse and then boil the beets in water until you can easily slip a fork or knife through them.

While the beets are boiling, sauté the garlic, carrots and shallot in olive oil until the shallot is translucent. Let cool. Also, if you are using cream, let it rest on the counter to room temperature.

When the beets are done, purée them and the cooked vegetables, and add it all, plus the wine and caraway to a soup pot of chicken stock; stir, cover and simmer for about fifteen minutes, stirring periodically. If it seems too thick for you, add a little vegetable stock or water.

Serve the soup in a bowl with a dollop of sour cream in the center, or, just before serving, turn out the flame under the pot and stir heavy cream into the soup.

Sprinkle with black pepper to taste and garnish with parsley.

Pasta

*T*HE WORD PASTA refers to paste that is made from grain—any grain. The following recipes are made from semolina wheat flour paste; but first, here is the best way to cook them.

About 2⅓ quarts of water is sufficient to cook 16 ounces of pasta. Instead of salt, try the juice of half a lemon in the water. Also, add a tbl. olive oil to keep the pasta from sticking; then bring the water to a roaring boil and add the pasta.

Pasta is best when it is slightly undercooked—the term in Italian is "al dente" or chewy yet pliable. Pasta needs an average ten minutes cooking time to become al dente, but that is an average based on dry pasta. Fresh pasta needs to be checked every few minutes while it cooks. As a general rule, it is good to check pasta for consistency as soon as the water it cooks in comes to its second boil.

PENNE REGATE WITH SMOKED SALMON

INGREDIENTS TO SERVE TWO
3 cloves garlic, chopped
1 shallot, chopped
2 tbl. olive oil (1 to keep pasta from sticking)
juice of half a lemon (for the pasta water)
16 oz. penne regate
2½ quarts water
⅓ pound smoked salmon, in small pieces
¼ cup of semi-dry Riesling
¼ cup dry Marsala
1 large sweet red pepper, roasted and sliced in small pieces*
1 cup of broccoli tips
handful of kalamata olives (pitted)
1 tsp. each chopped oregano and basil
crushed hot red pepper to taste
¼ cup freshly grated Romano cheese
½ cup chopped parsley

*For pepper roasting see chapter 9, ravioli with red and yellow pepper sauce

Cook the pasta as described earlier.

Sauté shallot in olive oil in a large pan until it becomes translucent; then add the garlic and sauté 30 seconds. Add the Riesling, broccoli tips and hot pepper. Cover and simmer under low heat for five minutes.

Add to the pan the cooked pasta, salmon, olives, roasted peppers, oregano, basil and Marsala. Mix well, and then turn off heat.

Serve in pasta bowls and sprinkle with grated Romano cheese and parsley garnish, in that order.

You can replace smoked salmon with anchovies, walnuts or toasted pine nuts. If you choose the pine nuts simply put them into a no-stick pan over medium flame and swirl them around while they toast for about five minutes, and then add them to the dish.

One of the greatest wines for this dish is Riesling. The three greatest places for Riesling production are Germany, Alsace and the Finger Lakes in New York. Of the three, New York produces the kind of fruity—yet dry—Rieslings that pair well with this dish. Of course, a fruity Pinot Grigio or Tocai Friuliano from the Alto Adige or Friuli-Venezia-Giulia regions, will do just fine, too.

The following is adapted from a Mediterranean fisherman's recipe that calls for pasta, fresh caught sardines and perhaps some spices that are on board the fishing vessel; it is also a favorite of our cat too, who loves a dose of sardine juice poured over her food.

PENNE REGATE WITH SARDINES
INGREDIENTS TO SERVE TWO
3 cloves garlic, minced
1 shallot, chopped
2 tbl. olive oil (1 for the pasta)
2½ quarts water
juice of ⅓ a lemon (for the water)
2 cans of sardines packed in water
½ cup Marsala plus a dash more
16 oz. of penne regate
1 large yellow tomato, diced

1 tbl. each basil and thyme
crushed hot red pepper to taste
1 oz. heavy cream
¼ cup grated Romano cheese
¼ cup chopped parsley

Cook the pasta.

Sauté the shallot in olive oil in a large pan until it is translucent; then add the garlic and sauté 30 seconds.

Chop the sardines and add them to the pan along with ⅓ cup wine, the thyme, ½ the basil and the tomato. Cover and simmer on low heat for about ten minutes, stirring a couple of times.

Just before serving, add the additional dash of Marsala and the heavy cream to the sauce; mix well. Serve in a bowl and garnish with grated Romano cheese, parsley and the rest of the basil.

Riesling will do well with penne and sardines, but so will a medium-bodied red wine; perhaps a northern Italian Dolcetto, a Chinon from the Loire in France, or Cabernet Franc from the Northeast of either Italy or the United States.

Sometimes you want a thick, rich pasta dish. None is thicker or richer than carbonaro.

PASTA CARBONARA
INGREDIENTS TO SERVE TWO
3 cloves garlic, pressed
2 tbl. olive oil (1 for the pasta)
2½ quarts water
juice of ½ a lemon (for the pasta water)
16 oz. fettuccine, linguini or spaghetti
½ cup dry Marsala
2 eggs
handful of pine nuts or chopped walnuts
½ cup heavy cream
1 tsp. chopped basil
½ cup grated Reggiano cheese

¼ pound pancetta or prosciutto, sliced into small pieces
ground black pepper to taste
¼ cup chopped parsley

Cook the pasta. Let the cream rest on the counter to get up to room temperature.

Sauté garlic in olive oil over low heat in a large pan for one minute.

If you are using pine nuts or walnuts add them to a small no-stick pan, over medium flame and swirl and flip for a few minutes, until they have toasted. Turn off the flame and let the nuts sit.

Deglaze the pan of garlic with Marsala and reduce to about one third.

Beat the eggs in a bowl—lightly—with a fork; count to forty and stop.

Drain the pasta and mix with the nuts and pancetta (or prosciutto) into the large pan of garlic and wine, let simmer for 2 minutes uncovered, stirring all the while.

Add the eggs, cream, grated cheese and parsley, turn off the flame and mix vigorously for a minute.

Serve in bowls with black pepper to taste.

Carbonara calls for white wine—big, creamy and fat. Try Chardonnay from either California or Australia, or deeply rich white from France's Burgundy, or a soft, rich white from Sicily.

Pasta in the Friuli region, in northeast Italy, sometimes refers to the ancient barley grain. The following is northeastern Italy's version of pasta e fagiole (macaroni and beans).

INGREDIENTS TO SERVE FOUR
8 cloves garlic, minced
2 shallots, chopped
1 tbl. olive oil
1 cup large-grain barley
6 oz. each cannellini, navy and red kidney beans
2 cups freshly made veal stock

1 tbl. each chopped basil, oregano and rosemary
1 cup dry Marsala
¼ cup freshly grated Reggiano cheese
ground black pepper to taste
handful of chopped parsley

If you are using fresh beans, you must first clean and then cook them in water with a touch of baking soda for half an hour, then strain them and rinse them twice. Canned beans are ready to use; just open the can and drain well. Dry beans have instructions on the package.

Soak and rinse the barley for two hours, then mix it with two cups of water in a pan, bring to a boil, lower flame and simmer until most of the water is absorbed (about ten minutes). Turn off the flame and cover.

Purée the cooked cannellini beans with ½ cup of veal stock (plus any pieces of veal that fell off the bone).

Sauté the shallot in olive oil in a large pan until it is translucent; then add garlic, basil, oregano, rosemary, cannellini purée, Marsala and the rest of the veal stock to the pan, cover and simmer for about twenty minutes.

Add the rest of the beans and the barley, mix and simmer for five minutes.

Serve with black pepper to taste and with parsley and grated cheese garnish.

The best wine pairing for this pasta e fagiole is Tocai Friuliano or Sauvignon Blanc that is also produced in northeastern Italy.

The following is the southern Italian version of
PASTA E FAGIOLE
INGREDIENTS TO SERVE TWO
3 cloves garlic, minced
2 tbl. olive oil (1 for the pasta)
2 quarts of water for the pasta
juice of ½ a lemon (for the water)
1 cup ditallini pasta

8 oz. of cannellini beans
crushed or diced tomatoes (about 10 ounces)
½ cup of strong Italian red wine
1 tbl. each chopped oregano, basil plus a bay leaf
crushed hot pepper to taste
½ cup freshly grated Reggiano cheese
¼ cup chopped parsley

Handle the beans as discussed in the previous recipe.

Sauté garlic in olive oil in a large pan for one minute, then add tomatoes, wine, half the oregano and basil, bay leaf and hot pepper. Cover and let simmer under low flame. Start to cook the pasta.

While you wait for the pasta to cook, add the beans to the pan. Stir and continue to simmer on low heat.

When the pasta is done, strain it, mix it with the rest of the basil and oregano and serve it in bowls; then pour the beans and sauce over it.

Garnish with grated Reggiano cheese and parsley, in that order.

Campania has been the seat of wonderful red wines for centuries, all of which will do nicely with this pasta e fagiole. But a particularly good wine for the dish comes from Puglia (Apulia) on the Adriatic shores; it is called Salice Salentino.

Rice

*M*Y MOTHER made the following dish often. She called it Spanish rice, and she used chicken instead of sausage.

INGREDIENTS TO SERVE TWO
3 cloves garlic, chopped
1 Spanish onion, chopped
2 tbl. olive oil
1 cup Basmati rice
1 cup chicken stock
¼ cup dry Marsala
4 chorizo (Latino sausage)
2 oz. tomato paste
½ cup chopped fresh cilantro leaves
1 green bell pepper, sliced
optional:
½ cup freshly grated Reggiano or ¼ pound of sliced mozzarella

Place the chorizo in an electric broiler (or oven) at 350 degrees to both cook and dry out: about 30 minutes.

Use a large pan so that you can add the other ingredients as you progress in the preparation. Sauté the onion in olive oil until it is translucent; then add garlic and sauté 30 seconds.

Bring the cup of rice to a boil in two cups of water; then simmer until just before the rice soaks up all the water (about ten minutes). Turn off the heat, cover and let sit.

Add half the cilantro and green pepper to the onion and garlic and cook with no cover for three minutes; then add the chicken stock to the pan and stir in the rice. Cover and let simmer, stirring frequently, for about fifteen minutes.

Take the sausage out of the broiler or oven and slice. When the rice has soaked up most of the chicken stock, but not all of it, add the sausage, wine and tomato paste and stir. Add the optional cheese on top. Turn off heat, cover and let sit for three minutes.

Garnish with the rest of the cilantro just before serving.

The Spanish produce marvelous red table wines. Wines from the Rioja, Penedes and Ribera del Duero regions are my favorites—look for Crianza or Reserva from those regions. Dry sherry also pairs well with this rice dish.

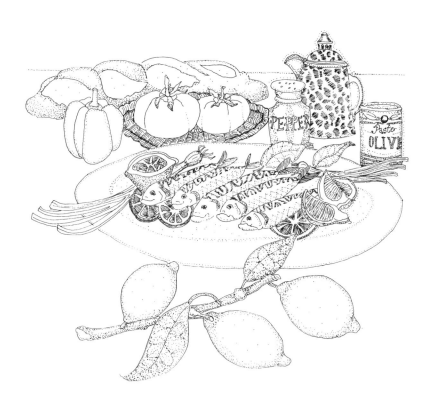

Seafood and Fish

*F*EW DINNERS are as pleasing and exotic as soft-shell crabs. The crabs are becoming scarce and expensive, but they are a must-have when they are in season during early summer.

INGREDIENTS TO SERVE TWO
3 cloves of garlic, chopped
3 tbl. olive oil
4 tbl. unsalted butter
4 medium-sized soft shells
1 cup milk
¾ cup all purpose flour
½ tsp. cayenne pepper
juice of 1 lemon.
1 large tomato, sliced ¼-inch pieces
handful of chopped parsley

Run water over the live crabs and clean thoroughly.

Heat the olive oil at medium in a large pan. Sprinkle the cayenne into the oil.

Spread the flour on a flat plate.

Dip one crab at a time into the milk and then dip into the flour, giving a light coating on both sides. The idea is to get just a dusting of flour to stick.

Sauté the crabs in olive oil and cayenne for two or three minutes on each side, or until golden brown. Remove from heat and drain in a colander over paper towels.

Heat the butter under low heat. Toss the garlic into the butter, swirling until the butter turns brown and begins to foam. Turn off the heat and squirt the lemon juice into the butter and garlic, mix.

Serve the crabs on a plate, pour the garlic butter over them; put a slice or two of tomato atop the crabs and garnish with parsley.

Dry, fruity, young and crisp Chardonnay or Sauvignon Blanc suits soft shells, or any other white wine meeting the description.

Mexican or Spanish restaurants often have the following cala-mari dish on their menu. It is rich and flavorful.

INGREDIENTS TO SERVE TWO
3 cloves garlic, minced
1 sweet onion, chopped
3 tbl. olive oil
4 large squid
½ cup Riesling, semi-dry
1 cup Basmati rice
crushed hot red pepper to taste
½ cup sweet peas
1 roasted sweet red pepper, sliced
¼ cup chopped parsley

Add the rice to two cups of water and bring to a boil. Then sim-mer until most of the liquid is absorbed. Cover and turn off heat to let the rice absorb the remaining water.

Clean and chop the calamari into little pieces. Cut the head from the body. Separate the tentacles from the head and put them aside.

Sauté garlic, onion and the hot pepper in olive oil in a large pan until the onion is translucent. Add the wine to the pan with the chopped calamari pieces and the tentacles, cover and simmer on low heat.

The rice should be ready by now; scoop it out of the pot and add it to the calamari, and add the peas, too. Then gather up the squid heads, one by one hold them over the pan and puncture the pocket behind the eyes to release the black ink. Mix all the black ink you have released into the rice and stir. Turn off the flame. Let stand a few minutes so that the rice becomes completely dry.

Serve the dish in a large soup bowl and garnish it with slices of roasted red pepper and chopped parsley.

If you haven't enough calamari ink to soak the rice in black, try adding a dash of concentrated raspberry or blueberry juice for color.

A difficult dish to pair with wine, because of its relative dry-ness and austere flavors. Perhaps a light fruity Pinot Noir, Gamay or northern Italian red.

Shad roe is available just a few weeks in early spring. It is sold in pairs of two sacks filled with the tiny roe. Little needs to be done to prepare the rich shad roe.

INGREDIENTS TO SERVE TWO
3 cloves garlic, minced
1 shallot, chopped
¼ cup Marsala
1 pair shad roe
2 tbl. unsalted butter
1 lemon
ground black pepper to taste
¼ cup chopped parsley

Sauté shallot in butter until it is translucent. Add the garlic, shad roe and wine over medium heat and do not cover. Cut the lemon in half and squirt one half over the roe. Cook on one side for three or four minutes, press down on the roe, then turn it over to cook another three or four minutes on the other side.

Slide the roe onto a plate with a spatula, then spoon out the garlic and the remaining cooking juices over the roe. Pepper to taste and garnish with parsley. Serve with a lemon wedge.

The richness of shad roe calls for a fruity wine like Pinot Noir, Beaujolais or Rosé.

Garlic, Wine and Olive Oil

Meats

$\mathcal{S}$WEETBREADS prove the adage that hard work produces satisfying rewards. You don't eat the membrane surrounding the tender, succulent sweetbreads. It's a tedious but necessary task to peel the membrane away. One way of doing it is to par-boil sweetbreads and then peel away at the membrane.

INGREDIENTS FOR MARINADE
3 cloves garlic, chopped
1 cup milk
½ pound sweetbreads

Put the garlic and sweetbreads into milk in a bowl and let stand for a few hours on the counter. An hour before cooking, take the sweetbreads out of the milk and put the milk aside. Press the sweetbreads under a weight of some sort (a brick) for an hour to remove all liquid.

INGREDIENTS TO SERVE TWO
3 cloves garlic, minced
1 shallot, chopped
3 tbl. olive oil
¼ cup chicken stock
¼ cup dry Marsala
½ cup white flour
1 egg
1 lemon
1 tbl. each chopped basil and parsley
ground black pepper to taste

Sauté shallot in 1 tbl. olive oil until it is translucent. Deglaze the pan with wine and let it reduce to a trace, then add garlic, chicken stock, basil and juice of a lemon to the pan and let it reduce to about ½ over medium heat.

Beat the egg in a bowl. Spread out the flour on a board. Dip the sweetbreads in the milk, roll them in the egg and then roll them in the flour for a fine coating.

Add the remaining olive oil to a separate pan over medium heat. Add the sweetbreads to the pan and cook on both sides until golden brown.

Serve the sweetbreads on a plate over which pour the reduced sauce, sprinkle pepper to taste and garnish with parsley.

This is another richly tasting recipe and would do nicely matched with fruity reds. But a fruity Riesling and Gewürztraminer can also stand up to sweetbreads.

CALVES' LIVER
INGREDIENTS FOR MARINADE
1 clove garlic, chopped
¼ cup milk
Marinate ½ pound of liver (two ¼ pound slices) in the milk and garlic for 24 hours, refrigerated.

INGREDIENTS TO SERVE TWO
3 cloves garlic, minced
1 onion, sliced
3 tbl. olive oil
2 marinated liver slices
½ cup Marsala or Madeira
2 pats of butter
¼ cup flour
1 tsp. each chopped thyme and basil
crushed black pepper to taste
2 lemon wedges
handful chopped parsley

Remove the liver from the milk and garlic, discard them and let the liver drip until dry. Then pepper each side of the liver and give each side a dusting of flour.

Heat 2 tbl oil to medium and then sauté the liver no more than

2 minutes on each side, which should be enough for the flour to become golden.

Remove the liver and place on a warm waiting plate or tray. Add the rest of the oil and the butter and cook the onion in it until it is translucent, then add the garlic, thyme and basil and sauté another minute or two.

Raise the heat to high and add the wine. Let the wine foam and cook until the liquid is reduced to half, stir everything up in the pan and turn off the heat.

Place the liver into serving dishes and pour and spoon out the sauce with onions over each. Sprinkle with black pepper to taste. Serve with a lemon wedge and a parsley garnish.

Southern Italian red, fruity Australian Shiraz or Pinot Noir wines are equally pleasing with calves' liver.

Being neither a fan of turkey nor its "fixings", I demanded one year that we have something different for Thanksgiving. I offered to do the cooking. The family took me up on my offer; the following is what they got.

MARINATED RACK OF LAMB

Marinate the rack in dry red wine with 2 cloves crushed garlic for at least 12 hours, at room temperature.

INGREDIENTS TO SERVE TWO
3 garlic cloves
(2 pressed for the marinade and 1 chopped for cooking)
1 rack of about eight ribs
1 cup red wine
2 tbl olive oil
pat of butter
1 tbl. rosemary leaves
a few mint leaves, plus some for garnish
1 tbl. crushed black pepper
4 tbl. quince jelly

Marinade the lamb in a bowl of pressed garlic and wine for a few hours before preparation.

Take the lamb out of the marinade and put aside to drain. Add to a small pot the wine marinade chopped clove of garlic, jelly, mint and rosemary and simmer over low heat—be careful not to boil it over. Just let the liquid reduce.

Turn on high flame under a cast iron skillet (use no oils or lubricants). Give the skillet time to heat up (3 minutes) then place the lamb in for about three minutes on one side, or until the lamb is easily lifted from the pan. Turn the lamb over to cook similarly on the other side.

Three minutes on each side gives you quite rare rack of lamb. If you want it cooked more, simply turn the lamb over one more time, cover the pan, turn off the flame and wait two or three minutes. The lamb will continue to cook.

Remove the lamb and set aside. Add olive oil and the butter to the pan, plus whatever remains of the marinade simmering in the pot, stir and cook down to about half the liquid.

Cut the rack in half, serve on a plate and pour the sauce over it. Top up with a sprinkle of ground pepper and a mint leaf garnish.

Try the lamb with a bold Pinot Noir (or Burgundy wine), an Australian Shiraz or a California Syrah or Zinfandel.

OSSO BUCO

The success of my Thanksgiving rack of lamb spawned a new tradition. My next foray into revolutionary Thanksgiving dinners was osso buco (braised veal shanks). The aroma of this dish as it braises in a casserole pot for two hours beats the aroma of turkey in the oven any day.

INGREDIENTS TO SERVE FOUR
Gremolata (the garnish):
1 tsp. minced garlic
1 tbl. grated lemon zest
¼ cup finely chopped parsley
The osso buco:

3 cloves garlic, chopped
4 tbl. unsalted butter
4 tbl. olive oil
3 carrots, diced
1 cup of diced tomatoes
1 onion, chopped
¼ pound prosciutto, diced
4 veal shanks, each a couple of inches thick
¼ cup white flour
⅔ cup dry Marsala
1⅓ cup beef stock
½ cup fresh peas
ground black pepper to taste

In a large casserole that can be tightly covered melt the butter over medium heat, uncovered. Add carrots, onion, garlic and prosciutto and stir frequently until the vegetables are tender, about ten minutes. Add tomatoes and raise the heat. Stir frequently until the liquid has evaporated. Remove from the heat.

Some recipes call for the veal to be tied with string, but the meat holds fairly well against the bone without having to be tied. Season the veal with pepper and dust it with flour, shaking off excess flour.

Heat the oil in a large skillet and then brown the veal on all sides.

Put the browned veal on top of the vegetable in the casserole and then add wine to the skillet where the veal browned. Simmer the wine until it reduces to half. Add the beef stock to the wine, stir, and then add the mixture to the casserole.

Cover the casserole and bring to a near boil over high heat. Turn down heat and cover tightly to simmer for about two hours.

When done, remove the meat and let it sit on a platter. Pass the ingredients in the casserole through a food mill (some throw out the solids that remain, I like to eat them as a side dish or save them for a soup stock). Put the veal back into the casserole, pour the sauce over the meat and simmer uncovered for about five minutes.

Cook the peas in boiling water for about three minutes. And then drain and put them aside.

Combine the minced garlic, lemon zest and parsley to make the gremolada, and put it aside.

Remove the veal and serve on plates, pouring a little sauce over each and then a garnish of peas topped with the gremolada.

Fruity, citric-like white wine—un-oaked Chardonnay, Pinot Grigio, Sauvignon Blanc—all do well with this dish.

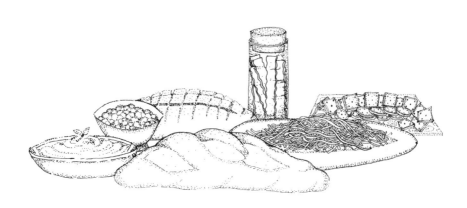

Garlic, Wine and Olive Oil

Vegetable Side Dishes

Tired of red meat; try the following recipe.

GRILLED PORTABELLO MUSHROOM

INGREDIENTS TO SERVE TWO
2 cloves of garlic, chopped
2 large portabello mushroom caps, sliced into ½-inch pieces
1 tbl. olive oil, plus a dribble
2 roasted sweet red peppers, sliced
Ground black pepper to taste

Sauté garlic in 1 tbl. olive oil for one minute in a cast iron pan.

A reasonably sized portabello should get you from eight to ten slices. It is important that the slices are thick. For effect, cut them on an angle.

Swipe a grill or grill pan with a little olive oil and place the mushroom slices on the grill or pan. Cook on one side until soft but not dry; then do the same on the other side.

Serve by placing alternating slices of mushroom and pepper across the plate—boy, girl, boy, girl style. Spoon out the garlic and sprinkle some over the mushroom and then sprinkle black pepper to taste.

Red Bordeaux, Cabernet Sauvignon, Cabernet Franc or Merlot will do nicely with grilled portabello.

Potatoes

GARLICKY SMASHED POTATOES
INGREDIENTS TO SERVE FOUR
4 cloves garlic, pressed
2 shallots, chopped
2 tbl. olive oil
1 pound new red potatoes
¼ cup milk
¼ cup chopped parsley
ground black pepper

Bring a pot of 2 quarts water to the boil. Cube the potatoes and boil them, in their skins, until you can stick a fork easily through them.

Sauté shallot in oil until it is translucent; then add garlic and sauté 30 seconds.

Mix the potatoes with the garlic and shallot, then smash the mixture with a fork, all the while slowly adding the milk. You want some of the potatoes mashed while the rest remain in whole chunks; you may not need all the milk.

Serve with a parsley garnish and black pepper to taste.

The wonderful river-fish dishes in Iran were often served with the following side dish.

HOME FRIED POTATOES
INGREDIENTS TO SERVE TWO
2 cloves garlic, chopped
1 tbl. olive oil
2 red potatoes
1 shallot
¼ cup Marsala wine
1 tbl. paprika
handful of chopped parsley
ground black pepper to taste

Garlic, Wine and Olive Oil

Sauté shallot in olive oil on medium heat until they are translucent.

Dice the potatoes into small cubes, leave the skins on and then put them and the garlic into the pan and cover for five minutes. Then add the wine, cover and simmer for five more minutes. Then lift the cover and move the potatoes around with a spatula, flipping them over in the process and then spread them evenly in the pan. Sprinkle paprika and half the parsley on top of the potatoes, cover and cook until done (when a fork glides through the potato). Just before serving, sprinkle with black pepper to taste, plus the rest of the parsley.

SLICED, FRIED POTATOES
INGREDIENTS TO SERVE TWO
2 cloves garlic, minced
2 large red potatoes
½ cup olive oil, plus some in reserve
salt
teaspoon of cayenne

Pour the oil into a large pan. Sprinkle a little cayenne into the oil. Turn the heat up high.

Slice the potatoes into thin, potato chip-like bits in your food processor, or as thin as you can get them by hand (leave the skins on). When the oil is hot (300) throw the garlic in and lay the round slices of potato in, side by side, until you fill the pan. The oil should cover the potato slices but they shouldn't drown in it.

Cook the potatoes on one side until golden, then flip and cook the other side until golden—it takes only a few minutes to do this. Some of the slices will puff with air, usually the thinner ones.

Lift the potatoes out, one at a time if need be, with a spatula, holding them to let the oil drip back into the pan. Place the potatoes in a strainer and hang it over paper towels to drain. Sprinkle salt, to taste, over the potatoes. If you hadn't gotten all the potatoes in on the first cooking, add a little more oil, get it hot, and do it all over again.

For a simple, yet pleasing, potato dish try this recipe I adapted from one my Hungarian sister-in-law prepares.

INGREDIENTS TO SERVE TWO
2 cloves garlic, chopped
2 large potatoes, quartered (with skins)
1 sweet onion, sliced thin
½ cup chopped parsley.
1 tbl. paprika
ground black pepper to taste.

Put the potatoes, onion and garlic into 2½ quarts of boiling water and cook until a fork slips easily into the potatoes.

The dish is done. Just serve the potatoes on a plate, topped up with paprika, parsley and pepper to taste.

A favorite dish when I was growing up, potatoes and eggs is both filling and tasty, and can serve as a main course.

INGREDIENTS TO SERVE TWO
2 cloves garlic, minced
2 pats butter
1 tbl. olive oil
1 large onion, sliced
2 large red potatoes, cut into cubes, with skins
6 eggs
dash of Tabasco sauce
¼ cut Marsala or Madeira
1 tsp. each tarragon and thyme
¼ cup mixed parsley and basil, chopped
1 roasted red pepper, sliced
crushed black pepper to taste

Sauté onion in 1 pat of butter and olive oil until it is translucent; then add garlic and sauté 30 seconds. Add the rest of the butter, the potatoes, ½ the wine, tarragon and thyme, cover and cook until potatoes are soft—add more wine as the liquid evaporates.

Garlic, Wine and Olive Oil

Break the eggs into a bowl, add a dash of water and a dash of Tabasco, and mix lightly with a fork to the count of forty. Add the eggs to the potatoes and let cook until the edges of the eggs firm up, then flip the whole mixture with a spatula and cook some more, until the eggs are solidified but still moist.

Serve on a plate with a garnish of fresh basil, parsley and pepper to taste, plus strips of roasted red pepper.

GRILLED VEGETABLES

can be cooked over charcoal or in a smoker.

INGREDIENTS TO SERVE TWO

3 cloves garlic, minced

3 tbl. olive oil

2 potatoes, quartered

1 onion, sliced

2 tiny Italian eggplants or 1 large eggplant, sliced

2 large portabello mushroom caps, sliced into ½-inch pieces

2 sweet red peppers, sliced

1 hot red pepper, chopped

2 tbl. each chopped basil, oregano, thyme and parsley

Some people find eggplant too bitter. To remove some of the bitterness, try sprinkling salt over uncooked sliced eggplant, let it rest a while and then wipe off the salt.

Brush each slice of potato and eggplant with olive oil and either bake them, plus the sweet red pepper, in the oven or smoke in a smoker, until the potato is firm outside and soft inside, the eggplant is soft and the pepper is soft. Watch the eggplant while baking or smoking so that it does not dry out—brush a little more oil if it starts drying.

Sauté the garlic, onion, mushroom and hot pepper in 2 tbl. olive oil with oregano, basil and thyme, until the onion is translucent.

When all the vegetables are cooked, put them together in a pan, add the remaining olive oil, mix and sauté for a couple more minutes.

Garnish with parsley and serve.

Escarole and broccoli were two of the most prevalent vegetables in our kitchen when I grew up. Broccoli rape was served too.

INGREDIENTS TO SERVE TWO
3 cloves garlic, chopped
2 tbl. olive oil
1 shallot, chopped
head of escarole or broccoli rape
¼ cup dry Marsala
handful of chopped oregano
juice of one lemon
1 tsp. sugar
ground black pepper to taste

Sauté shallot in oil in a large pan until it is translucent.

Add the garlic, escarole or broccoli rape, oregano, Marsala and sugar, cover and simmer for about ten minutes. Just before serving squirt a whole lemon all over the vegetable.

Serve with pepper to taste.

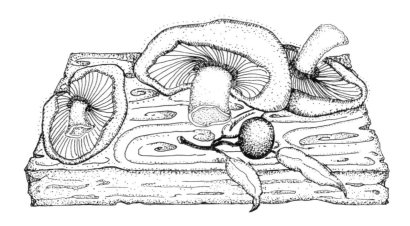

Garlic, Wine and Olive Oil

Salads

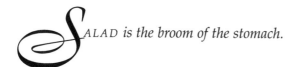

ALAD is the broom of the stomach.

—AN ITALIAN SAYING

S THEY MADE THE SHIFT from meat to plants, early civilizations must have eaten a variety of salads from their gardens. Knowing the primitive nature of winemaking at the time, they had a good supply of vinegar for their dressing too. Perhaps a couple of thousand years later, with the cultivation of olives, the dressings became the highlight of the salads.

Today, Anne and I save wine bottles into which we put homemade dressings. To cap the bottles we use plastic "slow pours", the kind used in wine tasting rooms to control the flow of wine. Two of our favorite salad dressings are the simplest of all.

1. INGREDIENTS
3 cloves garlic, pressed
Juice of 2 whole lemons
1 tbl. chopped basil
1/2 cup olive oil
cracked black pepper, to taste

Mix the ingredients and shake it all up; then splash on the salad.

2. INGREDIENTS
olive oil, two parts
balsamic or wine vinegar, one part
handful of chopped oregano, thyme and basil or other herbs.
cracked black pepper, to taste

Mix all and splash on the salad. Be creative with herbs.

A great way to extract the taste of fresh herbs is by steeping them in vinegar.

HERB VINEGAR WITH GARLIC
4 cloves garlic, chopped
white vinegar to fill the bottle
sprigs of herbs enough to fill the bottom third of the bottle

Place the garlic in a quart mason jar. Then take whole herb leaves and stuff them in the jar. Fill the jar with white vinegar. Cap and let the vinegar stand for at least a month and then pour the vinegar off, filter and store in a glass bottle.

Many people disdain pairing wine with salad, especially if the dressing includes vinegar. But if you create the right balance in the dressing, or if you use the delicate balsamic vinegar, you can match the dressing with a fine flowery, fruity, off-dry Riesling.

In Brooklyn, salad followed the main course, thereby ending the meal until dessert arrived. Since this book is not concerned with dessert, it is fitting that we end right here. I sincerely hope you know more about garlic, wine, and olive oil than you did when you opened the book, and that you had fun reading the story and then preparing the recipes. Now, take a look at the wine and food pairings in the following appendices, and perhaps get a hold of some of the books listed in the bibliography.

Garlic, Wine and Olive Oil

Appendix 1

Recipes in this book and their wine pairing.

RECIPE	WINE
INTRODUCTION:	
Recipe for Baked Garlic.	Riesling; Semillon; Vouvray
	White, fruity, crisp and clean.
CHAPTER 1	
Garlic Soup.	Dry Sherry; Dry Madeira (Verdelho)
	Fortified, hardy and full.
CHAPTER 2	
Persian melon with yogurt.	Rosé d'Anjou; White Zinfandel
	Light, fruity, off-sweet.
Caviar omelet.	Riesling
	White, fruity, crisp and clean.
Chellow kebab.	Shiraz; Syrah; Rhone red wine
	Red, peppery, lush and full.
CHAPTER 3	
Fish in olive oil.	Gamay; Rosé; Sparkling wine
	Red or pink, fruity and crisp
Calamari.	Sauvignon Blanc; Pinot Grigio
	White, dry, crisp and clean.
Wok cooking.	Gewürztraminer; Madeira (Bual)
	First is white, can be off-dry, spicy
	Second is fortified, luscious, nutty
CHAPTER 5	
Stuffed grape leaves.	Semillon; Tocai Friuliano
	White, fruity, crisp and clean.
CHAPTER 6	
Bread dipped in olive oil.	Dolcetto; Barberesca
	Red, light, medium acid.
CHAPTER 7	
Wedding Soup.	Riesling; Gewürztraminer OR
	Beaujolais; Chinon; Gamay
	White, dry, crisp, fruity, spicy OR
	Red, light, fruity.

Jugged hare.	Madeira Sercial; Dry Sherry *Fortified, hardy and full.*
CHAPTER 8 Survival package.	Barberesca; Chianti, Shiraz; Zinfandel, Crianza *Bold red wines*
CHAPTER 9 Spinach in olive oil.	Dry Riesling *White, fruity and crisp*
Meatballs.	Chianti; Refosco; Salice Salentino *Red, dry and bold.*
Zucchini flowers.	Chardonnay; Pinot Blanc *White, dry, crisp, clean*
Fish chowder.	Chianti; Rioja; Salice Salentino *Red, dry and bold.*
Pasta in tomato sauce	Chianti; Rioja; Salice Salentino *Red, dry and bold.*
Ravioli in pepper sauce.	Gewürztraminer; Riesling *White, dry, spicy.*
Rice and black beans.	Shiraz; Syrah; Ribera del Duero *Red, dry, bold.*
Risotto.	Pinot Grigio; Tocai Friuliano; Riesling *White, dry, fruity, crisp.*
Veal and sautéed broccoli.	Chardonnay; Pinot Blanc *White, dry, fruity.*
CHAPTER 10 Ravioli en brodo.	Pinot Grigio; Sauvignon Blanc *White, dry, fruity.*
CHAPTER 12 Soup.	Dry Madeira; dry sherry *Fortified, bold and dry*
Penne with smoked salmon.	Riesling; Pinot Grigio; Tocai Friuliano *White, dry, fruity, crisp*
Penne with sardines.	Dolcetto; Chinon; Cabernet Franc *Red, light and fruity*
Pasta carbonara.	Chardonnay; Burgundy & Sicilian white *White, soft and buttery*

Garlic, Wine and Olive Oil

Pasta e fagiole. (with barley)	Tocai Friuliano; Sauvignon Blanc
	White, fruity and crisp
Pasta e fagiole. (southern Italian)	Salice Salentino; Chianti
	Red, dry and bold
Spanish rice.	Crianza; Reserva; dry sherry
	Red and bold (sherry is fortified)
Soft shell crabs.	Chardonnay; Sauvignon Blanc
	White, dry, crisp and clean
Calamari in its ink.	Pinot Noir; Gamay; Refosco
	Red, dry, fruity, delicate
Shad roe.	Pinot Noir; Beaujolais; Rosé
	Red or pink, fruity and bright
Sweetbreads.	Riesling; Gewürztraminer
	Dry, fruity, spicy
Calves' liver.	Rhone; Shiraz; Sicilian red
	Dry, bold and forward
Rack of lamb.	Burgundy; Shiraz; Syrah; Zinfandel
	Red, big and bold
Osso buco.	Pinot Grigio; Chardonnay; Sauvignon Blanc
	White, fruity and crisp

Appendix 2

Various wines to match recipes in this book; by grape variety,
unless otherwise noted.

NOTE: This listing refers only to chapters and recipes in this book. It is not a comprehensive list of worldwide wines or grape varieties.

White wine	Description	Chapter	Recipe
Chardonnay	*Dry and crisp and clean*	9	Zucchini Flowers
		9	Veal Cutlets
		12	Pasta carbonara
		12	Soft shell crabs
		12	Osso buco
Gewürztraminer	*Dry and spicy*	3	Wok cooking
		7	Wedding soup
		9	Ravioli in pepper sauce
		12	Sweetbreads
Pinot Grigio	*Dry, crisp and clean*	3	Calamari
		9	Risotto
		10	Ravioli/Tortellini en brodo
		12	Penne with smoked salmon
		12	Osso buco
Pinot Blanc	*Dry and fruity*	9	Zucchini flowers
		9	Veal cutlets
Riesling	*Fruity, crisp and clean*	Intro	Baked garlic
		2	Caviar omelet
		7	Wedding soup
		9	Spinach in olive oil
		9	Ravioli in pepper sauce
		9	Risotto
		12	Penne with smoked salmon
		12	Sweetbreads
Sauvignon Blanc	*Dry, crisp and clean*	3	Calamari
		10	Ravioli/Tortellini en brodo
		12	Pasta e fagiole (with barley)
		12	Soft shell crabs
		12	Osso buco
Semillon	*Fruity, crisp and clean*	Intro	Baked garlic
Tocai Friuliano	*Fruity and crisp*	5	Stuffed grape leaves
		9	Risotto
		12	Penne with smoked salmon
		12	Pasta e fagiole (with barley)
Vouvray (primary grape Chenin Blanc)	*Fruity and crisp*	Intro	Baked garlic

Other white wines

Dry sparkling wine	3	Fish in olive oil
Sicilian dry white and dry white Burgundy	12	Pasta carbonara

Red wine

Barberesca   *Light, medium acid*
(primary grape Nebiollo)

6	Bread dipped in olive oil
8	Survival package

Chianti   *Dry and bold*
(primary grape Sangiovese)

8	Survival package
9	Meatballs
9	Pasta in tomato sauce
9	Fish chowder
12	Pasta e fagiole (tomato sauce)

Chinon   *Light and fruity*
(primary grape Cabernet Franc)

7	Wedding soup
12	Penne with sardines

Dolcetto   *Light, medium acid*
(primary grape Nebiollo)

6	Bread dipped in olive oil
12	Penne with sardines

Gamay (grape)   *Light, fruity and crisp*
(also Beaujolais, region)

3	Fish in olive oil
7	Wedding soup
12	Calamari in its ink
12	Shad roe

Pinot Noir (grape) *Dry, fruity or delicate*
(also Burgundy, region)

12	Calamari in its ink
12	Shad roe
12	Rack of lamb

Refosco   *Dry and fruity*

9	Meatballs
12	Calamari in its ink

Shiraz (grape)   *Dry, peppery and full*
(also Syrah, grape or Rhone, region)

2	Chellow kebab
8	Survival package
9	Rice, black beans and pork
12	Calves' liver
12	Rack of lamb

Zinfandel   *Big and bold*   12   Rack of lamb

Other red wines

Salice Salentino   *Dry and bold*
(Southern Italian)

9	Meatballs
9	Pasta in tomato sauce
9	Fish chowder
12	Pasta e fagiole (tomato sauce)

Sicilian dry   *Bold*   12   Calves' liver

Spanish	*Dry and bold*		
(Crianza or Reserva, most regions)		8	Survival package
		9	Rice, black beans and pork
		9	Pasta in tomato sauce
		9	Fish chowder
		12	Spanish rice

Rosé or pink

d'Anjou	*Dry, fruity and delicate*	2	Persian melon
		3	Fish in olive oil
		12	Shad roe
White Zinfandel	*Fruity with sweetness*	2	Persian melon

Fortified

Dry sherry	*Hardy and full*	1	Garlic soup
		7	Jugged hare
		12	Soup
		12	Spanish rice
Dry Madeira	*Hardy and full*	1	Garlic soup
		7	Jugged hare
		12	Soups
Semi-dry Madeira	*Luscious and nutty*	3	Wok cooking

Garlic, Wine and Olive Oil

Appendix 3

Recent gardening and cultivation books for garlic, grapes, and olives.

Garlic

Coonse, Marian. *Onions, Leeks and Garlic: A Handbook for Gardeners.* Texas A&M University Press, 1995.

Engelland, Ron. *Growing Great Garlic: Definitive Guide for Organic Gardeners and Small Farmers.* Filaree Productions, 1995.

Grapes

Cox, Jeff. *From Vine to Wines: The Complete Guide to Growing Grapes and Making Your Own Wine.* Storey Books, 1999.

Reichwaye, Randall, ed. *The American Wine Society Presents Growing Wine Grapes;* GW Kent, 1994.

Olives

Dolamore, Anne. *The Essential Olive Oil Companion.* Interlink Publication Group, 1993.

Rosenblum, Mort. *Olives: The Life and Lore of a Noble Fruit.* North Point Press, 1996.

Footnotes

PART I—THE ANCIENT PERSPECTIVE

1. Harris, Lloyd J. *The Book of Garlic*. New York: Holt, Rhinehart and Winston, 1975. p. 44.
2. Ibid. p. 72
3. Ibid. p. 14
4. Ibid. p. 11
5. Ibid. p. 32
6. McNutt, Joni G. *In Praise of Wine*. Santa Barbara: Capra Press, 1993. p.45.
7. Lichine, Alexis. *Alexis Lichine's Encyclopedia of Wines & Spirits*. New York: Knopf, 1967. p. 1.
8. Hyams, Edward. *Dionysus*. New York: MacMillan, 1965. p.36.
9. Klein, Maggie Blythe. *The Feast of the Olive*. Berkelely: Harris, 1983. p. 60.
10. Rosenblum, Mort. *Olives*. New York: Northpoint Press, 1996. p. 217.
11. Tannerhill, Reay. *Food In History*. New York: Stein and Day, 1973. p. 312.

PART II—CLASSICAL GREECE AND ROME

1. Harris. *Book of Garlic*. p. 20.
2. Tannerhill. *Food In History*. p. 95.
3. Harris. *Book of Garlic*. p. 29.
4. Gibbon, Edward. *Decline and Fall of the Roman Empire*. New York: Random House, Modern Library Edition. p. 1.
5. Harris,. *Book of Garlic*. p. 39.
6. Tannerhill. *Food In History*. p. 219.
7a. McNutt. *In Praise of Wine*. p. 48.
7b. Roden, Claudia . *A Book of Middle Eastern Food*. New York: Vintage, 1974. p. 35.
8. McNutt. *In Praise of Wine*. p. .50.
9. Root, Waverly. *Food of Italy*. New York: Vintage, 1977. pp. 102-107.
10. Ibid. pp. 120-121.
11. McNutt. *In Praise of Wine*. p. 68.
12. Ibid. p. 90.
13. Rosenblum. *Olives*. p. 49.
14. Klein, Maggie Blythe. *The Feast of the Olive*. Berkeley: Harris, 1983. p. 28.

PART III—AGE OF DISCOVERY TO NINETEENTH CENTURY

1. Harris. *Book of Garlic*. p. 63.
2. Jones, Evan. *American Food*. New York: E.P. Dutton, 1975. p. 91.
3. McNutt,. *In Praise of Wine*. p. 108.
4. Grossman, Anne and Thomas, Lisa Grossman. *Lobscouse & Spotted Dog*. New York: W.W. Norton, 1997. p. 176.
5. Root. *The Food of Italy*. p. 92.

PART IV—JOURNEY'S END

1. Tannerhill. *Food In History*. p. 85.

PART V—TO YOUR HEALTH

1. Harris. *Book of Garlic*. p. 25.
2. Ibid. p.30

PART VI—PERSONAL RECIPE FAVORITES

1. McNutt. *In Praise of Wine*. p. 78.

Bibliography

Allen, H. Warner. *A History of Wine*. New York: Horizon Press, 1961.

Andrews, Colman. *Flavors of the Riviera*. New York: Bantam, 1996.

Berolzheimer, Ruth, ed. *Culinary Arts Institute Encyclopedic Cookbook*. Processing and Books, Inc. 1971

Braudel, Fernand. *Mediterraneans and the Mediterranean World in the Age of Philip II*. New York: Harper & Row, 1949.

Braudel, Fernand. *Structure of Everyday Life: Civilization & Capitalism, 15th-18th Century*. New York: Collins & Harper and Row, 1981.

Brown, Gordon. *Handbook of Fine Brandies*. New York: MacMillan, 1990.

Crawford, Stanley. *A Garlic Testament*. New York: HarperCollins, 1992.

Croft-Cooke, Rupert. *Madeira*. London: Putnam, 1961.

Croft-Cooke, Rupert. *Port*. London: Putnam, 1957.

Croft-Cooke, Rupert. *Sherry*. London: Putnam, 1955.

Fisher, MFK. *The Art of Eating*. New York: World Publishing, 1954.

Flandrin, Jean-Louis et al. *Food: A Culinary History*. Columbia University Press, 1999.

Gabler, James M. *Passions: Wines & Travels of Thomas Jefferson*. Baltimore: Bacchus, 1995.

Gabler, James M. *Wine Into Words*. Baltimore: Bacchus Press, 1985.

Gibbon, Edward. *Decline and Fall of the Roman Empire*, New York: Modern Library/ Random House.

Grossman, Anne and Thomas, Lisa Grossman. *Lobscouse & Spotted Dog*. New York: Norton, 1997.

Harris, Lloyd J. *The Book of Garlic*. New York: Panjandrum Press, 1975.

Harris, Lloyd J. *The Official Garlic Lovers Handbook*. Berkeley: Aris, 1986.

Hyams, Edward. *Dionysus*. New York: MacMillan, 1965.

Jones, Evan. *American Food*. New York: E.P. Dutton, 1975.

Klein, Maggie Blythe. *The Feast of the Olive*. Berkeley: Harris Publishing, 1983.

Knickerbocker, Peggy. *Olive Oil From Tree to Table*. San Francisco: Chronicle, 1997.

Kramer, Samuel Noah. *History Begins at Sumer*. Philadelphia: University of Pennsylvania Press, 1981.

Lesko, Leonard H. *King Tut's Wine Cellar*. Berkeley, 1977.

Lichine, Alexis. *Alexis Lichine's Encyclopedia of Wines & Spirits*. New York: Knopf, 1967.

Lutz, H.F. *Viticulture and Brewing in the Ancient Orient*. New York: Leipzig, 1922.

Mariani, John. *Dictionary of Italian Food*. New York: Broadway Books, 1998.

McNutt, Joni G. *In Praise of Wine*. Santa Barbara: Capra Press, 1993.

Miller, J. Innes. *Spice Trade of the Roman Empire: 29 BC to 641 AD*. Oxford, 1969.

Pinney, Thomas. *A History of Wine in America: From the beginnings to prohibition*. University of California Press, 1989.

Reed, Howard S. *A Short History of the Plant Sciences*. New York: The Ronald Press, 1941.

Roden, Claudia. *A Book of Middle Eastern Food*. New York: Vintage, 1974.

Root, Waverly. *Food*. New York: Simon & Schuster, 1980.

Root, Waverly. *The Food of Italy*. New York: Vintage, 1977.

Rosenblum, Mort. *Olives*. New York: North Point Press, 1996.

Rosengarten, David and Wesson, Joshua. *Red Wine With Fish*. New York: Simon & Schuster, 1989.

Seward, Desmond. *Monks and Wine*. New York: Crown, 1979.

Simkin, C.G.F. *The Traditional Trade of Asia*. London and New York: 1968.

Stark, Freya. *Alexander's Path*. New York: Harcourt, Brace & World, 1958.

Tannerhill, Reay. *Food In History*. New York: Stein and Day, 1973.

Tousaint-Samat, Maguelonne. *A History of Food*. Blackwell Publishers, 1994.

Tuchman, Barbara W. *A Distant Mirror*. New York: Knopf, 1978.

Unwin, Tim. *Wine and the Vine*. London: Routledge, 1991.

Veyne, Paul et al. *A History of Private Life: From Pagan Rome to Byzantium*. Boston: Harvard University Press, 1987.

Vitale, Gioletta. *Riso*. New York: Crown, 1992.

Index of Recipes

SOUP

Beet 188, 189

Chicken 183

Escarole 184

Garlic 25, 26

Lentil 185

Pea 186

Potato and Leek 186, 187

Pumpkin-Curry 187, 188

Ravioli in broth (en brodo) 153

Soup stock 180, 181

Tortellini in broth 153

Wedding soup 100

GRAINS

Bread, dipped in olive oil 91

Pasta carbonara 192, 193

Pasta in tomato sauce 135, 136

Pasta with beans (pasta e fagioli) 193-195

Penne with salmon 190, 191

Penne with sardines 191, 192

Ravioli in pepper sauce 138, 139

Rice, Spanish 196, 197

Rice and black beans with pork, 141, 142

Risotto (Italian rice) 143, 144

MEATS

Chicken breast (cooked in a wok) 63

Hare, jugged 103

Lamb (rack), 203, 204

Lamb (chellow kebab) 47, 48

Liver (calves') 202, 203

Notes